An Anthology of Nineteenth-Century Women's Poetry from Spain

Texts and Translations

The Texts and Translations series was founded in 1991 to provide students and teachers with important texts not readily available or not available at an affordable price and in high-quality translations. The books in the series are intended for students in upper-level undergraduate and graduate courses in national literatures in languages other than English, comparative literature, ethnic studies, area studies, translation studies, women's studies, and gender studies. The Texts and Translations series is overseen by an editorial board composed of specialists in several national literatures and in translation studies.

For a complete listing of titles, see the last pages of this book.

An Anthology of Nineteenth-Century Women's Poetry from Spain

In English Translation, with Original Text

Introduction by
Susan Kirkpatrick

Edited by
Anna-Marie Aldaz

Translated by
Anna-Marie Aldaz and
W. Robert Walker

The Modern Language Association of America
New York 2009

Library of Congress Cataloging-in-Publication Data

An anthology of nineteenth-century women's poetry from Spain in English translation, with Spanish text / introduction by Susan Kirkpatrick; edited by Anna-Marie Aldaz; translated by Anna-Marie Aldaz and W. Robert Walker.
p. cm. — (Texts and translations)
Includes bibliographical references.
ISBN 978-1-60329-028-9 (paperback : alk. paper)
1. Spanish poetry—Women authors. 2. Spanish poetry—19th century.
3. Spanish poetry—Women authors—Translations into English.
4. Spanish poetry—19th century—Translations into English.
I. Aldaz, Anna-Marie, 1944- II. Walker, W. Robert, 1943- III. Title: Anthology of 19th century women's poetry from Spain in English translation, with Spanish text.
PQ6177.A64 2008
861′.50809287—dc22 2008039644

Texts and Translations 23
ISSN 1079-252x
ISSN 1079-2538

Cover illustration:
Santiago Rusiñol, *Alegoría de la Poesía*. Paris, 1894–95.
Museo Cau Ferrat, Sitges, Spain. © 2008 Artists Rights Society (ARS), New York / VEGAP, Madrid. Photograph copyright: Photographic Archive of the Consortium of Sitges's Patrimony

Printed on recycled paper

Published by The Modern Language Association of America
26 Broadway, New York, New York 10004-1789
www.mla.org

CONTENTS

INTRODUCTION

In 1846, a young Spanish woman wrote a letter to the editor of a periodical titled *El defensor del bello sexo* ("Defender of the Fair Sex"), to justify a new phenomenon:

> La cuestión de si las jóvenes *deben o no dedicarse a hacer versos* nos parece ridícula. La *poetisa* existe de hecho y necesita cantar, como volar las aves y correr los ríos, si ha de vivir con su índole natural, y no comprimida y violenta. Considérenla sus defensores y sus contrarios como un *bien* o un *mal* para la sociedad, pero es inútil que decidan si debe o no existir porque no depende de la voluntad de los hombres.
> (Coronado, "Al Sr. Director" 97)

> The question of whether young women *should write verse or not* seems to us ridiculous. The *woman poet* exists in fact and must sing, just as birds fly and rivers flow, if she is to live in accord with her innate nature and not in violent repression. Her defenders and her adversaries may consider her *good* or *bad* for society, but it is futile for them to decide whether she should exist or not, because that does not depend on men's will. (my trans.)

The author of these words was Carolina Coronado, one of a small group of women poets who had begun to publish poetry in Spain in the early 1840s. Her combative tone suggests the novel and controversial nature of this incursion of Spanish women into the territory of print culture.

In other parts of Europe, women writers had become well-established and successful producers of almost every genre for the literary market in the eighteenth century, but in Spain, where less than ten percent of women were literate by the end of that century, very few women had ventured into print, and most of them had done so in the role of translator rather than as original author. In the first four decades of the nineteenth century even fewer works by women saw print, above all because of the effects on the Spanish publishing industry of the six-year war against the Napoleonic invasion, which ravaged the Peninsula from 1808 to 1814 and was followed by the draconian repression of the press under the regime of Ferdinand VII, the restored absolutist monarch, who reigned from 1815 to 1832. After his death, the publishing industry rebounded and began to expand rapidly, developing new markets, new genres, and new producers. It was in this context that women who, like Coronado, came of age in the 1840s, found the stimulus and the opportunity to write for the public. From that decade forward, women writers gained an increasingly important place in the Spanish literary world. A recent bibliographic study has 4,752 entries for publications by women in the nineteenth century, all except a handful dating from after 1840 (Simón Palmer). This number may be small compared with that of female-authored publications in England or the United States during the same period, but it is significant in relation both to the previous dearth of such publications in Spain and to the total production of the Spanish press.

It is interesting, from the perspective of the present anthology, that the preponderance of works by Spanish women printed in the mid–nineteenth century belonged to the genre of lyric poetry, a genre that had rarely been cultivated by eighteenth-century female authors. As time went on, more and more women writers shifted with notable success to fiction, to essays, and even to theater, but virtually all of them launched their careers with a book of lyric poetry. A clue to the reason for this preference can be found in Coronado's assertion that singing is as natural to women as flying is to birds. The assumption that lyric poetry is a kind of spontaneous overflow of feeling was a basic tenet of Romanticism, a movement that reached its apogee in Spain around 1840—that is, precisely at the beginning of the decade in which Spanish women began to publish poetry in significant numbers. The logic of this conjunction becomes clear when we consider that even privileged women of the time had little access to literary education in a country where feminine literacy was viewed as at best unnecessary and at worst a path to immorality. In this context, the Romantic belief that a poem's value derives from its expression of emotion and imagination rather than from the skill with which it applies the principles of an aesthetic tradition (learned through long schooling in classical literature) served as a basis on which women with no schooling could stake a claim as poets. In the scheme whereby Spanish culture (and European culture in general) ascribed distinguishing natural characteristics to the two sexes, emotion and a certain kind of fanciful imagination were clearly feminine properties. The diffusion of the Romantic aesthetic in mid-century Spain, then, encouraged women to think that their emotional spontaneity could compensate for their lack of education and give them legitimacy and value as poets. It even allowed them to imply, as Coronado did in her letter to the editor, that women were poets by nature.

Of course, as Coronado's letter also implies, this view encountered plenty of adversaries, no doubt more adversaries than defenders. If women's reading was taboo for a broad sector of the Spanish public, women's writing was even worse—a threat to society and to the fundamental order of things represented by the hierarchical relationship between men and women. In traditional Spain, a family's honor depended on the public invisibility and silence of its women. The consequence of these attitudes was, in Coronado's view, the "violent repression" that impeded women's natural need to express themselves. In the same letter Coronado refers to the sad fate of women who, because of old-fashioned prejudices, were not allowed the release of expressing their thoughts. She thus implicitly links her justification of women's writing to another movement that was profoundly affecting Spanish society at the time: liberal reform.

Since the beginning of the century, Spanish liberals (Coronado's male relatives among them) had been engaged in a bloody struggle to rid the country of its traditional regime of aristocratic privilege and absolute monarchy. Although the conflict-ridden endeavor to establish a stable liberal system would continue through the century, by 1840 the liberals had enacted a legal reform that eliminated seigneurial rights, transformed estates and entailments into private property, and installed a moderately liberal constitutional monarchy. Liberal ideology advocating the rights of the individual was gaining ground against more traditional ideas about social hierarchies. Freedom of expression was a right dear to liberals in a country in which the alliance between church and state had had a particularly repressive effect on free thought since the sixteenth century. Although no Spanish women of the period conceived of proposing, as Mary Wollstonecraft and Olympe de Gouges had done, that the rights of men should also be the rights of women, the concept of a right to self-expression through imaginative writing did embolden women who had aspirations to share in some form of intellectual life beyond the home. Coronado deftly plays on liberal assumptions in presenting the denial of the possibility of writing poetry as a violent form of repression, while assuring her public that a woman poet was no more threatening than a singing bird.

If claiming that the right to express emotions and perceptions was grounded in their nature as women provided these nineteenth-century Spanish poets with a justification for writing, it also exacted a price. Their poetry, to be taken as the expression of a spontaneous femininity, had to conform to contemporary ideas about women's basic nature. The view that women's social role and psychological makeup were determined by their biological function as childbearers was taking root in Spain as in the rest of Europe at this time. True womanhood was identified with the ideological image of the angel of the house—a maternal, altruistic, sexless, sensitive, and spiritual (or, in Spain, devout) figure. This version of authentic feminine subjectivity exercised a powerful constraint on mid-century women poets, preventing them from exploring the full range of Romantic subjectivity expressed in the work of their male contemporaries. Cynicism, anger, rebelliousness, sexual passion, arrogance, religious doubt, political dissidence—modalities closely associated with Romantic poetry—could be evoked only in attenuated and disguised forms by these women, if they wished to be identified as truly feminine (and thus justified in writing) poets.

The literary models adopted by the poets represented in this anthology reflect the pressure of social norms. For the most part rejecting the rebellious Byronic strain of Romantic poetry, these writers looked to more conservative and idealizing precedents for themes and poetic vocabularies. One of the most important models was the sentimentalizing tradition of eighteenth-century Spanish rococo poetry, whose refined diction, delicate exploration of feeling, and idealization of reality were highly compatible with the nineteenth-century model of feminine subjectivity. Another important influence was the early work of the French Romantic poet Alphonse Lamartine. It modeled a personalized discourse of feeling closely associated with religious devotion, a discourse that Spanish women could adapt—appropriately, in the eyes of their society—for self-expression.

The poetry of nineteenth-century Spanish women evolved in different directions in the course of first asserting its right to exist and then finding the configuration best suited to the needs and desires of its practitioners and readers. The poetry written in the 1840s by the three pioneers of the women's tradition, Josefa Massanés, Gertrudis

Gómez de Avellaneda, and Carolina Coronado, often employs defensive rhetorical strategies, such as false modesty, to ward off hostile responses from a public unaccustomed to seeing women appear in print. Though they were preoccupied with the issue of their right and authority as poets, Gómez de Avellaneda and Coronado in particular explored expressive avenues that later poets would abandon. Gómez de Avellaneda measured herself against Europe's most prestigious male Romantic poets by translating and writing poems explicitly in the manner of Lord Byron (George Gordon), Victor Hugo, and Lamartine. She also ventured a few poems about the passions of heterosexual love. Coronado, emboldened by the success of her first book of poetry (1843), wrote a series of what we might call protofeminist poems that called attention to the oppressive conditions shared by women in a supposedly liberalizing society. Sometimes indirectly, sometimes not, both poets express anger, ambitious desires, and passion.

From the 1850s and through the 1870s, however, the range of expression by women poets became more restricted as the ideal of the domestic angel became the dominant feminine norm in Spanish society. In 1857, Coronado herself confirmed this trend. In an article on Spanish women writers, she repented of her "infantiles" ("childish") verses lamenting women's enslavement and asserted that women needed now to be in their homes rather than in academies in order to preserve the family and with it the nation's well-being ("Galeria"). This ideological turn was reinforced by the development of the publishing industry, which by this time had established a clearly delimited niche devoted to women readers. Poetic production by women was subsumed in this niche, along with domestic fiction, conduct books, religious tracts, sewing instructions, fashion plates—all dominated by the sign of the domestic angel. Direct expression of nonangelic modes of feeling such as anger, erotic love, and personal ambition all but disappeared from women's poetry during these decades, but there were many poignant expressions of internal conflict and of the difficulty of maintaining conformity.

By the end of the century, the dominant model for women's poetry was beginning to collapse. As Spanish society modernized and new aesthetic models such as naturalism and then modernism replaced Romanticism, the forms and language that had come to represent the spontaneous expression of feminine subjectivity seemed vacuous and artificial rather than authentic. The great poet Rosalía de Castro was the first to break out of the straitjacket of the feminine tradition that had formed. While accepting the idea of women's destiny as suffering and sacrifice, Castro probed this psychic territory more deeply and discovered new possibilities for poetic expression. But by the end of the century, the possibilities of the tradition that had begun with Coronado were exhausted. Finding it no longer necessary to justify their writing as the outflow of spontaneous feminine feeling, twentieth-century Spanish women were free to find different identities and missions as poets. The texts included in this anthology, however, bear witness to the struggles and achievements of their forerunners and bring alive the first engagement of Spanish women as a group in the process of literary self-representation.

Works Cited

Coronado, Carolina. "Al Sr. Director." *El defensor del bello sexo* 8 Feb. 1846: 96–97.

———. "Galería de poetisas españolas contemporáneas: Introducción." *La discusión* 1 May 1857: 3.

Simón Palmer, María del Carmen. *Escritoras españolas del siglo XIX: Manual biobibliográfico*. Madrid: Castalia, 1991.

WORKS CONSULTED

Primary Sources

Acuña, Rosario de. *Ecos del alma*. Madrid: A. Gómez Fuentenebro, 1876.

Arenal de Carrasco, Concepción. "La esclavitud de los negros." *Cancionero del esclavo: Colección de poesías laureadas y recomendadas por el jurado en el certamen convocado por la Sociedad Abolicionista Española*. Ed. Sociedad Abolicionista Española. Madrid: Sociedad Abolicionista Española, 1866. 18–22.

———. *Fábulas en verso originales*. Madrid: H. Reneses, 1854.

Armiño, Robustiana. *Poesías*. 2 vols. Oviedo: Martínez Hermanos, 1851.

Bautista y Patier, Eladia. *Poesías*. Madrid: Juan José de las Heras, 1870.

Biedma, Patrocinio de. *Guirnalda de pensamientos: Poesías*. Barcelona: Luis Tasso, 1872.

Cambronero, Manuela. *Días de convalecencia: Colección de poesías y novelas originales*. La Coruña: Domingo Puga, 1852.

Casanova, Sofía. *Poesías*. Madrid: Aurelio J. Alaria, 1885.

Castro, Rosalía de. *Obras completas*. Ed. Manuel Arroyo Stephens. 2 vols. Madrid: Turner, 1993.

Coronado, Carolina. *Poesías*. Madrid: Alegría y Charlain, 1843.

———. *Poesías*. Madrid: Fernández de los Ríos, 1852.

Estevarena, Concepción. *Últimas flores*. Sevilla: Gironés y Orduña, 1877.

Fenollosa, Amalia. *Poesías: Amalia Fenollosa, 1825–1869*. Ed. and introd. Santiago Fortuño Llorens. Valencia: Institució Alfons el Magnànim, Diputació de Valencia, 2002.

Gómez de Avellaneda, Gertrudis. *Poesías*. Madrid: Establecimiento Tipográfico, 1841.

———. *Poesías*. Madrid: Delgrás Hermanos, 1850.

Grassi, Ángela. *Poesías*. Madrid: Trujillo Hijo, 1871.

León, Rogelia. *Auras de la Alhambra: Poesías*. Granada: José María Zamora, 1857.

Massanés, Josepa. *Antología poética: Josefa Massanés i Dalmau*. Ed. and introd. Ricardo Navas Ruiz. Madrid: Castalia, 1991.

———. *Poesías*. Barcelona: J. Rubió, 1841.

Moreno Morales, Eduarda. *Ayes del alma*. Granada: Higueras y Otero, 1857.

Ríos de Lampérez, Blanca de los. *Esperanzas y recuerdos*. Madrid: Víctor Saiz, 1881.

Sáenz de Tejada, Victorina. *Poesías*. Granada: Otero y Compañía, 1865.

Sáez de Melgar, Faustina. *La lira del Tajo*. Madrid: Bernabé Fernández, 1859.

Sinués, María del Pilar. *Flores del alma*. Barcelona: Narciso Ramírez, 1860.

Ugarte Barrientos, Josefa. *Poesías selectas*. Málaga: La Ibérica, [1904].

Vázquez de Aldana, Enrique, ed. *Safo en Castilla: Antología de más de doscientas poetisas españolas, en sonetos ortodoxos*. Madrid: Studium de Cultura, 1953.

Secondary Sources

Caballé, Anna, ed. *La pluma como espada*. Barcelona: Lumen, 2004. Vol. 3 of *La vida escrita por las mujeres*.

Castilla, Alberto. *Carolina Coronado de Perry: Biografía, poesía e historia en la España del siglo XIX*. Madrid: Beramar, 1987.

Coronado, Carolina. *Obra poética: Edición, notas y estudio preliminar*. Ed. Gregorio Torres Nebrera. 2 vols. Mérida: Regional de Extremadura, 1993.

———. *Poesías*. Introd. and ed. Noël Valis. Madrid: Castalia; Instituto de la Mujer, 1991.

Davies, Catherine. *Spanish Women's Writing, 1849–1996*. London: Athlone, 1998.

Escoriaza, Teresa de, ed. *Antología*. Madrid: Sordomudos, 1929.

Flores, Angel, and Kate Flores, eds. *Poesía feminista del mundo hispánico, desde la Edad Media hasta la actualidad: Antología crítica*. Mexico: Siglo Veintiuno, 1984.

Fontanella, Lee. "Mystical Diction and Imagery in Gertrudis Gómez de Avellaneda and Carolina Coronado." *Latin American Literary Review* 9 (1981): 47–55.

Galerstein, Carolyn L., ed. *Women Writers of Spain: An Annotated Bio-bibliographical Guide*. Westport: Greenwood, 1986.

García de Enterría, María Cruz, ed. *Fábulas en verso originales: Concepción Arenal*. Madrid: Castalia, 1995.

Ginebra, Jordi. *Antoni de Bofarull i la Renaixença*. Lleida: Virgili & Pagès, 1988.

Gómez de Avellaneda, Gertrudis. *Antología: Poesías y cartas amorosas*. Ed. Ramón Gómez de la Serna. Buenos Aires: Espasa-Calpe, 1943.

———. *Antología poética*. Ed. Mary Cruz. Havana: Letras Cubanas, 1983.

———. *Poesías selectas*. Ed. Benito Varela Jácome. Barcelona: Bruguera, 1986.

———. *Poesías y epistolario de amor y amistad*. Ed. Elena Catena. Madrid: Castalia, 1989.

Gómez de la Serna, Ramón. "Mi tía Carolina Coronado." *Biografías completas*. Madrid: Aguilar, 1959. 869–980.

Harter, Hugh A. *Gertrudis Gómez de Avellaneda*. Boston: Twayne, 1981.

Jiménez Faro, Luzmaría, ed. *Panorama antológico de poetisas españolas (Siglos XV al XX)*. Madrid: Torremozas, 1987.

———, ed. *Poetisas españolas: Antología general*, tomo I: *Hasta 1900*. Madrid: Torremozas, 1996.

Kirkpatrick, Susan, ed. *Antología poética de escritoras del siglo XIX*. Madrid: Castalia, 1992.

———. "Gertrudis Gómez de Avellaneda, Carolina Coronado y Rosalía de Castro: Estudios recientes." *Ínsula: Revista de letras y ciencias humanas* Dec. 1989: 12–13.

———. *Las Románticas: Women Writers and Subjectivity in Spain, 1835–1850*. Berkeley: U of California P, 1989.

Levine, Linda Gould, Ellen Engelson Marson, and Gloria Feiman Waldman, eds. *Spanish Women Writers: A Bio-bibliographical Source Book*. Westport: Greenwood, 1993.

López, Aurora, and Andrés Pociña, eds. *Rosalía de Castro: Documentación biográfica y bibliografía crítica, 1837–1990*. 3 vols. [La Coruña]: Fundación Pedro Barrié de la Maza, 1991–93.

López López, Aurora. "Safo como referente de las poetas hispanas en los siglos XIX y XX." *Florentia iliberritana* 8 (1997): 221–41.

Manso Amarillo, Fernando. *Carolina Coronado: Su obra literaria*. Badajoz: Departamento de Publicaciones de la Diputación de Badajoz, 1992.

Martín, Elvira. *Tres mujeres gallegas del siglo XIX: Concepción Arenal, Rosalía de* Castro, *Emilia Pardo Bazán*. Barcelona: Aedos, 1977

Mayoral, Marina, ed. *Escritoras románticas españolas*. Madrid: Fundación Banco Exterior, 1990.

Miller, Beth. "Gertrudis the Great: Avellaneda, Nineteenth-Century Feminist." *Women in Hispanic Literature: Icons and Fallen Idols*. Ed. Miller. Berkeley: U of California P, 1983. 201–14.

McNerney, Kathleen, and Cristina Enríquez de Salamanca, eds. *Double Minorities of Spain: A Bio-bibliographic Guide to Women Writers of the Catalan, Galician, and Basque Countries*. New York: MLA, 1994.

Ontaña, Juana. *Doña Concepción Arenal como poeta*. Madrid: Arte Gráficas, 1932.

Peña, Pedro de la. *Antología de la poesía romántica*. Madrid: Júcar, 1984.

Pérez, Janet. *Modern and Contemporary Spanish Women Poets*. New York: Twayne, 1996.

Pinyol i Torrents, Ramon. "Les escriptores catalanes vuitcentistes i la traducció." *Quaderns: Revista de traducció* 13 (2006): 67–75.

Reina, Manuel Francisco, ed. *Mujeres de carne y verso: Antología femenina en lengua española del siglo XX*. Madrid: La Esfera de los Libros, 2002.

Rokiski Lázaro, Gloria. *Bibliografía de la poesía española del siglo XIX*. Vol 1: 1801–50. Madrid: Consejo Superior de Investigaciones Científicas, 1988.

Romo Arregui, Josefina, and Diana Ramírez de Arellano. *Poetas románticos desconocidos: Concepción de Estevarena, 1854–1876*. Madrid: Librería Internacional de Romo, 1979.

Simón Palmer, María del Carmen. *Escritoras españolas del siglo XIX: Manual bio-bibliográfico*. Madrid: Castalia, 1991.

Urrutia, José. *Poesía española del siglo XIX*. Madrid: Cátedra, 1995.

Valis, Noël M. "La autobiografía como insulto." *Actas del congreso de la Asociación Internacional de Hispanistas* 10 (1989): 325–42.

———. "The Language of Treasure: Carolina Coronado, Casta Esteban, and Marina Romero." *The Feminine Mode: Essays on Hispanic Women Writers*. Ed. Valis and Carol Maier. Cranbury: Bucknell UP, 1990. 246–72.

Vidal, María Antonia, ed. *Cien años de poesía femenina española e hispanoamericana, 1840–1940*. Barcelona: Olimpo, 1943.

Translations

Bankier, Joanna, ed. *Twentieth-Century Women's Poetry in Translation*. New York: Norton, 1976.

Barnstone, Alikai, and Willis Barnstone, eds. *A Book of Women Poets, from Antiquity to Now*. New York: Schocken, 1980.

Burnshaw, Stanley. *The Poem Itself*. New York: Holt, Rhinehart, 1960.

Castro, Rosalía de. *Beside the River Sar*. Trans. S. Griswold Morley. Berkeley: U of California P, 1937.

———. *Poems*. Trans. Anna-Marie Aldaz, Barbara N. Gantt, and Anne C. Bromley. New York: State U of New York P, 1991.

———. *Poems of Rosalía de Castro*. Trans. C. David Ley. Madrid: Ministry of Foreign Affairs, 1974.

Coronado, Carolina. "The Lost Bird." Trans. William Cullen Bryant. *The Poetical Works of William Cullen Bryant*. Ed. Henry C. Sturges. New York: Appleton, 1929. 236–37.

Flores, Angel, ed. *An Anthology of Spanish Poetry from Garcilaso to García Lorca*. Garden City: Anchor, 1961.

Flores, Angel, and Kate Flores, eds. *The Defiant Muse: Hispanic Feminist Poems from the Middle Ages to the Present: A Bilingual Anthology.* New York: Feminist, 1986.

———, eds. *Spanish Poetry / Poesía española: A Dual-Language Anthology, Sixteenth–Twentieth Centuries.* Mineola: Dover, 1998.

Kaminsky, Amy Katz, ed. *Water Lilies / Flores del agua: An Anthology of Spanish Women Writers from the Fifteenth through the Nineteenth Century.* Minneapolis: U of Minnesota P, 1996.

Nims, John Frederick. *Sappho to Valéry: Poems in Translation.* New Brunswick: Rutgers UP, 1971.

On Translation

Arrowsmith, William, and Roger Shattuck, eds. *The Craft and Context of Translation.* New York: Doubleday, 1964.

Barnstone, Willis. *The Poetics of Translation: History, Theory, Practice.* New Haven: Yale UP, 1993.

Bly, Robert. *The Eight Stages of Translation.* Boston: Rowan Tree, 1983.

De Beaugrande, Robert. *Factors in a Theory of Poetic Translating.* Assen, Neth.: Van Gorcum, 1978.

Eco, Umberto. *Mouse or Rat: Translation as Negotiation.* London: Weidenfeld, 2003.

Frawley, William, ed. *Translation: Literary, Linguistic, and Philosophical Perspectives.* Newark: U of Delaware P, 1984.

Hervey, Sándor G. J., Ian Higgins, and Louise M. Haywood. *Thinking Spanish Translation: A Course in Translation Method, Spanish to English.* London: Routledge, 1995.

Honig, Edwin. *The Poet's Other Voice: Conversations on Literary Translation.* Amherst: U of Massachussets P, 1985.

Landers, Clifford E. *Literary Translation: A Practical Guide.* London: Multilingual Matters, 2001.

Schulte, Rainer. *The Geography of Translation and Interpretation: Traveling between Languages.* Lewiston: Mellen, 2001.

Schulte, Rainer, and John Biguenet, eds. *The Craft of Translation.* Chicago: U of Chicago P, 1989.

———, eds. *Theories of Translation: An Anthology of Essays from Dryden to Derrida.* Chicago: U of Chicago P, 1992.

Weissbort, Daniel. *Translating Poetry: The Double Labyrinth.* London: Macmillan, 1989.

Reference Works

Casares, Julio. *Diccionario ideológico de la lengua española.* Barcelona: Gili, 1977.

Catalan Dictionary: English-Catalan, Catalan-English. London: Routledge, 1994.

Franco Grande, Xosé Luis. *Diccionario galego-castelán.* 8th ed. Vigo: Galaxia, 1983.

Martínez Amador, Emilio. *Diccionario inglés-español, español-inglés.* Barcelona: Sopena. 1964.

Navarro Tomás, Tomás. *Arte del verso.* Madrid: Visor Libros, 2004.

———. *Métrica española: Reseña histórica y descriptiva.* 7th ed. Barcelona: Labor, 1986.

NOTE ON THE TEXT

Spanish Versification

Unlike English meter, which is determined by the number of stressed syllables, or feet, Spanish poetic meter is based on syllabic count. Certain rules governing Spanish pronunciation, however, make counting poetic syllables more complicated than merely counting the number of vowels.

In the Spanish language, vowels are classified as weak (*i*, *u*) or strong (*a*, *e*, *o*). When a weak vowel merges with any other vowel, the resulting diphthong is counted as one syllable (e.g., *vial*, *huir*). But if a written accent on the weak vowel turns it into a strong vowel, each vowel becomes a separate syllable (*ví-a*, *hu-í*). Each strong vowel forms a separate syllable, which means that a word like *po-e-ta* has three syllables.

The syllable count is also influenced by the elision Spanish speakers make when one word ends in a vowel and the next word begins with a vowel. This linkage of vowels, known as synalepha in poetry, occurs with all vowels, weak or strong; it is not blocked by the silent *h* and can span more than two words. The following line from Concepción de Estevarena, for example "Fulguraba una luz junto a una pluma," has fourteen vowels but equals eleven syllables:

1	2	3	4	5	6	7	8	9	10	11
Ful/	gu/	ra/	ba-u/	na/	luz/	jun /	to-a-u/	na/	plu/	ma

The determination of syllables also depends on where the accentual stress falls in the last word of a line. Most Spanish words are accented on the penultimate syllable. If a verse ends in a so-called *palabra llana* (*se**ma**na*, ***cár**cel*), the syllabic count is not altered. If, on the other hand, it ends in a *palabra aguda*, a word that is stressed on the final syllable (*a**mor***, *le**ón***), a syllable is added. With the least frequent *verso esdrújul*, a line ending with a *palabra esdrújula*, a word that is stressed on the antepenultimate syllable (*para**dó**jico*, ***rá**pido*), a syllable is subtracted. For example:

Verso agudo (Moreno Morales): "ardiente como el seno del volcán" yields 10+1=11 syllables.

Verso esdrújul (Castro): "el vivo resplandor de los relámpagos" yields 12−1=11 syllables.

The most frequent lines in Spanish poetry are those with seven, eight, or eleven syllables. The *octosílabo* (eight-syllable line), which belongs to the so-called *versos de arte menor* (from two to eight syllables), was first used in medieval ballads, and it has remained the most popular Spanish verse form ever since. Octosyllabic verse is well represented in the poetry of Carolina Coronado, Gertrudis Gómez de Avellaneda, Amalia Fenollosa, and Concepción Estevarena, to mention a few.

Overall, however, nineteenth-century poets preferred the *versos de arte mayor* (nine or more syllables), especially the *endecasílabo* (eleven-syllable line). Of Italian origin, the *endecasílabo* was used most typically in sonnets, a form favored by many of the women poets, with the notable exception of Rosalía de Castro. In some standard verse forms, such as the *silva, madrigal, canción,* and *lira,* the *endecasílabo* is combined with the *heptasílabo* (seven-syllable line). An instance of an unusual combination can be seen in Rosario Acuña's poem "¡Poetisa!," which uses *decasílabo* (ten-syllable) and *tetrasílabo* (four-syllable) lines.

Rhyme is common in Spanish poetry, because, unlike English, which has relatively few rhyme words, Spanish abounds with them. As has been said somewhat tongue in cheek, the challenge in Spanish is to avoid rhyming (Landers 98). The two types of rhyme are *rima consonante* ("full rhyme"), when the vowels as well as consonants from the last stressed vowel onward share a sound, and *rima asonante* ("assonant rhyme"), when only the vowels match. Most Romantic poets preferred the richness of *rima consonante*, but some women poets, especially Castro, opted for *rima asonante*, which would become the modernists' rhyme of choice.

Work Cited

Landers, Clifford E. *Literary Translation: A Practical Guide.* London: Multilingual Matters, 2001.

Chronology of Poems

1841 María Josepa Massanés
"La resolución"
"El beso maternal"
"El velo perdido"
Poesías. Barcelona: Rubió

Gertrudis Gómez de Avellaneda
"Al partir"
"Imitación de Petrarca"
"A las estrellas"
"A una mariposa"
"A él" (fragmento)
"Mi mal"
Poesías de la Señorita Doña Gertrudis Gómez de Avellaneda. Madrid: Calle del Sordo 11

1843 Carolina Coronado
"A una gota de rocío"
"El pájaro perdido"
"El marido verdugo"
"El salto de Leucades"
"La rosa blanca"
"A una coqueta"
"Canción" [1]
"Canción" [2]
Poesías de la Señorita Doña Carolina Coronado. Madrid: Alegría y Charlain

1844 Robustiana Armiño
"Plegaria"
El Anfitrión Matritense 60

1845 Robustiana Armiño
"La tempestad"
Pensil del bello sexo: Colección de poesías, novelitas, biografías, artículos, etc. escrita por las señoras

Amalia Fenollosa
"Soneto"
Pensil del bello sexo

1848 Amalia Fenollosa
"A un ángel"
El Fénix: Periódico universal, literario y pintoresco 4

1849 Amalia Fenollosa

"Un adiós"

El album de las bellas: Periódico quincenal de ciencias, literatura, artes y modas, dedicado al bello sexo, por una Sociedad de Jóvenes sin nombre literario

"Mis celos"

El Celtíbero: Periódico de literatura 16

1850 Gertrudis Gómez de Avellaneda

"Soneto imitando una oda de Safo"

"El recuerdo importuno"

"A la luna"

"Al destino"

"A ***"

"Significado de la palabra *yo amé*"

"Romance"

Poesías de la excelentísima Señora Doña Gertrudis Gómez de Avellaneda. Madrid: Delgrás Hermanos

1851 Ángela Grassi

"La despedida"

Ellas: Órgano oficial del sexo femenino 4

Concepción Arenal

"El hierro y el topacio"

"La rosa y la espina"

Fábulas en verso originales. Madrid: Fortanet

1852 Carolina Coronado

"El espino"

"¡Primavera invisible!"

"Gloria de las flores"

"Bendito seas, Alberto"

"¡Oh, cuál te adoro!"

"Siempre tú"

"¡No hay nada más triste que el último adiós!"

"Nada resta de ti"

"Amistad de la luna"

Poesías de la señorita Doña Carolina Coronado. Madrid: Fernández de los Ríos

Manuela Cambronero

"La cautiva"

Días de convalecencia: Colección de poesías y novelas originales. La Coruña: Domingo Puga

1857 Rogelia León
"Una española a su amante"
Auras de la Alhambra: Poesías. Granada: José María Zamora

Eduarda Moreno Morales
"Safo"
Ayes del alma. Granada: Higueras y Otero

1859 Faustina Sáez de Melgar
"La primavera"
"El estío"
"El otoño"
"El invierno"
La lira del Tajo. Madrid: Bernabé Fernández

1860 María del Pilar Sinués
"Amor materno"
Flores del alma. Barcelona: Narciso Ramírez

1860–81 María Josepa Massanés
"Als bons pagesos i proletaris del Empordà"
"Grats recorts"
"Mon derrer viatge"
Poesies. Barcelona: Ilustració Catalana

1862 Rosalía de Castro
"Quíxente tanto, meniña, ..."
El album de la caridad

1863 Rosalía de Castro
"Pasa, río, pasa, río, ..."
Cantares gallegos. Vigo: D. J. Compañel

1865 Victorina Sáenz de Tejada
"La inconstancia"
Poesías. Granada: Otero y Compañía

1866 Concepción Arenal
"La esclavitud de los negros"
Cancionero del esclavo: Colección de poesías laureadas y recomendadas por el jurado en el certamen convocado por la Sociedad Abolicionista Española. Madrid: Sociedad Abolicionista Española

1870 ELADIA BAUTISTA Y PATIER
"A un pájaro"
Poesías. Madrid: Juan José de las Heras

1872 PATROCINIO DE BIEDMA
"La muerte"
Guirnalda de pensamientos: Poesías. Barcelona: Luis Tasso

1876 ROSARIO DE ACUÑA
"¡Poetisa!"
Ecos del alma. Madrid: Gómez Fuentenebro

CONCEPCIÓN ESTEVARENA
"Enigma"
El correo de la moda: Periódico del bello sexo: Modas, literatura, bellas artes, teatros, etc. 26

1877 CONCEPCIÓN ESTEVARENA
"La pluma del genio"
"Hojas y seres"
"Una hora"
Últimas flores. Sevilla: Gironés y Orduña

1880 ROSALÍA DE CASTRO
"¡Adiós¡"
"Rico ou probe, algún día..."
"Cada noite, eu chorando pensaba..."
"¿Quen non xime?"
"O pazo de A***"
"Estranxeira na súa patria"
"Tecín soia a miña tea, ..."
"Sempre pola morte esperas, ..."
"¿Por que?"
"Tan soio"
Follas novas: Versos en gallego. Madrid: Aurelio J. Alaria

1881 BLANCA DE LOS RÍOS
"La hoja blanca"
Esperanzas y recuerdos. Madrid: Víctor Saiz

1884 ROSALÍA DE CASTRO
"Era la última noche"
"Del mar azul las transparentes olas"

"Ansia que ardiente crece"
"De este mundo en la comedia"
"Sed de amores tenía"
"Glorias hay que deslumbran"
"¡Oh gloria!"
En las orillas del Sar. Madrid: Ricardo Fé

1885 Sofía Casanova
"Anhelo"
Poesías. Madrid: Aurelio J. Alaria

1904 Josefa Ugarte Barrientos
"Saffo"
Poesías selectas. Málaga: La Ibérica

NOTE ON THE TRANSLATION

This anthology features twenty-one of the more than forty women poets in Spain who published a book of poetry between 1841 and the turn of the century. Prominence is given to the three major nineteenth-century figures: Carolina Coronado, Gertrudis Gómez de Avellaneda, and Rosalía de Castro. Most of the poems contained here are not readily accessible in Spanish, and few have ever been available in English.[1]

The selections were chosen primarily for their aesthetic qualities, historic significance, and probable appeal to modern readers, as well as to illustrate prevalent themes in nineteenth-century feminine poetry. In many of the lyric poems, the feminine poetic voices confide their pervasive sense of melancholy and solitude to flowers, insects, birds, stars, and especially the moon. Among the most recurrent causes for sorrow are unrequited love, nostalgia, lost illusions, or the thought of death. Several poets protest, more or less explicitly, against gender inequality, and those who are fervent advocates of liberal reform denounce slavery and all forms of social inequity.

The anthology opens with "La resolución" ("Resolution"), an important poetic manifesto in which the Catalan poet María Josepa Massanés satirizes society's negative reaction to feminine authors and defends a woman's right to write. Massanés, who was bilingual, wrote this poem, as well as those contained in her first two poetry collections, *Poesías* (1841) and *Flores marchitas* (1850; "Wilted Flowers"), in Castilian.

Massanés's native Catalan, which like all of Spain's regional languages had been eclipsed by Castilian, experienced a resurgence during the nineteenth century. The rebirth of Catalan as a literary language, known as the Renaixença ("Renaissance"), was greatly furthered by the publication of Antoni de Bofarull's *Los trovadors nous* (1858; "New Troubadours"); by the publication of Víctor Balaguer's *Los trovadors moderns* (1859); and, above all, by the restoration in 1859 of Barcelona's traditional poetic contest, the Jocs Florals ("Floral Games").

For Massanés, who contributed two poems to Bofarull's anthology and participated in the Jocs Florals, these events were a turning point. From the 1860s onward, she wrote in her native language, even translating one of her best-known poems, "El beso maternal" ("A Mother's Kiss"), into Catalan.[2] She was instrumental in her region's linguistic revival, and even though her poems written in Catalan were not compiled until after her death, in *Poesies* (1908), they appeared in newspapers. Two of her most fervently nationalistic poems are "Les dones catalanes" ("Catalan Women"), in praise of Catalonian women, and "La roja barretina catalana" ("The Red Catalan Cap"), which helped turn the typical Catalan peasant's cap into a symbol of Catalonian pride.

In some of the excerpts included here from *Poesies*, Massanés's love for her homeland is expressed in a more intimate style that is reminiscent of Castro. Like Massanés, Castro played an invaluable role in the rebirth of her region's vernacular, especially since Galician had declined even more than Catalan as a literary language and was considered merely a dialect. With the appearance of her *Cantares gallegos* (1863; "Galician Songs"), the first book-length publication in Galician in centuries, and her second volume of poems, *Follas novas* (1880; "New Leaves"), Castro greatly advanced the cause of the Rexurdimento ("Renaissance"), the attempt by her husband, Manuel Murguía, and by other Galician intellectuals to restore their native language to its former splendor.

For the English translator, the regional languages, which require translation even in Spain, represent an additional challenge in the already difficult—many would say impossible—task of translating poetry. In this undertaking, we were guided by the notion that the best translation of a poem is another poem, which, ideally, would flow smoothly in English but without deviating too much from the original's essential form and content.

Illustrative of our desire to find a balance between extreme fidelity and excessive freedom is the decision not to imitate the prevalent end rhymes but to compensate for this loss by imposing a syllabic count on our translations. Even when the number of syllables does not equal that of the Spanish poem, it reflects the original's line lengths and is internally consistent. At times, we opt for an exact correspondence, as in "Romance" ("Ballad"), by Gertrudis Gómez de Avellaneda, where we copy the eight-syllable line, the most popular verse form in Spanish prosody and typical in ballads.

While a translation should undoubtedly preserve some of the original's historical flavor, it must speak to today's readers. For this reason, we do not adhere to the inverted word order favored by some nineteenth-century women poets, including Avellaneda, Coronado, and occasionally even Castro. We felt that in English, a language that is considerably less flexible in its syntax than Spanish, these baroque hyperbatons would sound particularly unnatural today. In our version of Avellaneda's "A la luna" ("To the Moon"), we also restore a natural word order to her stanza that is based on these lines from Lord Byron's "Sun of the Sleepless!": "That show'st the darkness thou canst not dispel, / How like art thou to joy remember'd well!":

> ¡Oh, cuánto te semejas
> de la pasada dicha
> al pálido recuerdo, que del alma
> sólo hace ver la soledad sombría!

> Oh, you resemble
> that pale memory
> of past happiness that exposes
> the somber solitude of the soul!

A comparison between our translation of Coronado's "El pájaro perdido" ("The Lost Bird") and William Cullen Bryant's version shows that he imitates the alternating seven-syllable and eleven-syllable verses of Coronado's *lira* with six-syllable and ten-syllable lines, and we opt for five and nine. More significant, Bryant's decision to replicate the end rhymes forces Bryant to pad his verses slightly by adding, "I know not where" and "I pray":

¡Huyó con vuelo incierto
y de mis ojos ha desaparecido!...
    Mirad si a vuestro huerto,
    mi pájaro querido
niñas hermosas, por acaso ha huido.

Bryant's translation:
My bird has flown away,
Far out of sight has flown, I know not where.
    Look in your lawn, I pray,
    Ye maidens, kind and fair,
And see if my beloved bird be there. (236)[3]

Our translation:
He fled from my sight,
flying away with unsteady wings.
    Lovely girls, see if
    my belovèd bird
perchance has landed in your garden.

It has been said that every generation needs its own translation, and our attempt throughout the anthology has been to capture the original's quaintness without sounding outmoded.

Notes

[1] Three known exceptions are a nineteenth-century version of María Josepa Massanés's "El beso maternal" (but our attempts to locate that translation have been unsuccessful) and excerpts from her poem "La resolución." The third is a translation of Coronado's "El pájaro perdido" by the American poet, editor, and translator William

Cullen Bryant (1794–1878). Bryant's "The Lost Bird" first appeared in the *Evening Post*, the New York newspaper he edited, and it is included in his 1929 *Poetical Works* (236–37). As this anthology was going to press, a new translation appeared of Castro's poems, including five featured here: "¡Adiós!," "Cada noite," "¿Quen no xime?," "Era la última noche," and "De este mundo."

[2] It appeared in *Lo gay saber* 1 (1868): 31 (Pinyol i Torrents 73).

[3] In 1857, the American poet visited Coronado in Madrid, and in his notes to "The Lost Bird" he comments favorably on the advent of women authors in Spain and adds, "One of the most remarkable of these, as a writer of both prose and poetry, is Carolina Coronado de Perry" (415). Bryant concludes his biographical sketch of Coronado, in which he praises her both as a person and as a writer, by saying, "Amid the duties of a wife and mother, which she fulfills with exemplary fidelity and grace, she has neither forgotten nor forsaken the literary pursuits which have given her so high a reputation." Among Coronado's prose works, Bryant calls attention to the novel *Jarilla* (1850), which he describes as "a beautiful story, full of pictures of rural life in Estremadura," and he remarks, "[It] deserves, if it could find a competent translator, to be transferred to our language" (417). In 1869, Bryant translated the novel himself and published installments of his translation in the *New York Ledger*, beginning on 30 October 1869 (Castilla 243n16).

Works Cited

Bryant, William Cullen. *The Poetical Works of William Cullen Bryant*. Ed. Henry C. Sturges. New York: Appleton, 1929.

Byron, George Gordon. "Sun of the Sleepless!" *Byron's Poetical Works*. Vol. 1. *Project Gutenberg*. 1 Sept. 2005. 4 Jan. 2008 <http://www.gutenberg.org/etext/8861>.

Castilla, Alberto. *Carolina Coronado de Perry: Biografía, poesía e historia en la España del siglo XIX*. Madrid: Beramar, 1987.

Castro, Rosalía de. *Rosalía de Castro: Selected Poems*. Trans. Michael Smith. Exeter, Eng.: Shearsman, 2007.

Massanés, María Josepa. "La resolución." Trans. Robert L. Smith and Judith Candullo. *The Defiant Muse*. Ed. Angel Flores and Kate Flores. New York: Feminist, 1986. 32–35.

Pinyol i Torrents, Ramon. "Les escriptores catalanes vuitcentistes i la traducció." *Quaderns: Revista de tradducció* 13 (2006): 67–75.

An Anthology of Nineteenth-Century Women's Poetry from Spain

María Josepa Massanés
(1811–87)

María Josepa Massanés i Dalmau
María Josefa Massanés i Dalmau

The Catalan poet María Josepa Massanés was one of the first women in the nineteenth century to publish a collection of poems. Her *Poesías* appeared in 1841, the year often considered to mark the beginning of book publication by women poets in that century. Her poetic manifesto, "La resolución" ("Resolution"), defends women who have artistic and intellectual aspirations, while her more traditional poem "El beso maternal" ("A Mother's Kiss") sings the praises of maternal love. This paean to motherhood enjoyed great popularity during Massanés's lifetime, and the New York State Board of Education encouraged public schools to add the English version of the poem to their list of recommended reading. In "El velo perdido," the lost shawl of the title is a metaphoric allusion to a young girl's loss of innocence, and Massanés resorts to the typically feminine poetic convention of casting the poem in the form of a confession.

Massanés's love of her native region and its language are especially apparent in her poems written in Catalan. Filled with patriotic pride, the speaker in "Als bons pagesos i proletaris del Empordà" ("To the Worthy Peasants and Laborers of Empordà") asks the audience rhetorically why hearing songs sung in Catalan causes such a strong emotional impact. She urges them to thank God for having Catalan blood and for the honor of being allowed to wear Catalonia's emblematic red cap. In the bucolic poem "Grats recorts" ("Fond Memories"), the poet apostrophizes the Segre River, extolling its beauty and that of the Catalonian landscape along its course.

La resolución

(selecciones)

¿Qué yo escriba? No por cierto,
no me dé Dios tal manía,
antes una pulmonía;
primero irme a un desierto.

Antes de componer quiero
tener por esposo un rudo,
mal nacido, testarudo,
avariento y pendenciero.

. . . .

¿Escribir yo? ¡Cielo santo!
Mal me quiere usted, D. Juan.
¿Olvida usté el que dirán
y a *cuánto me expongo, a cuánto*?

¡Oh!, no habrá quien me convenza,
bien puede usted argüir.
¿Una mujer escribir
en España? ¡Qué vergüenza!

¿Pues no se viera en malhora
que la necia bachillera
hasta francés aprendiera?
¿Ha de ir de embajadora?

Resolution

(excerpts)

Me write? Certainly not!
Save me from such mania—
let me catch pneumonia
or go to the desert.

Sooner than versify,
I'd marry a husband
who's ill-bred and stubborn,
greedy and pugnacious.

. . . .

Me write? Heaven forbid!
Don Juan, you wish me ill:
you know what they'll say and
the risk I'd be taking?

No, you can't convince me,
no matter what you say:
a woman write in Spain?
What a terrible shame!

They would look askance at
the silly bluestocking
who learns French. To be an
ambassador perchance?

Antes, Señor, las muchachas
no estudiaban ni leían,
ni en toda su vida oían
esas palabras *gabachas*.

. . . .

Pues como digo, Señor,
las muchachas no estudiaban,
pero en cambio cual fregaban…
… ¡Barrían con un primor!

Hilaban como la araña,
amasaban pan, cernían,
y apuesto que no sabían
si el Godo invadió o no España.

¿Qué le importa a la mujer
de dó se exporta el cacao;
si es pesca o no el bacalao
como lo sepa cocer?

. . . .

Y usted, amigo, quisiera
que una niña el canto alzara?
¿Qué yo en metro?… La pagara
bien cara si tal hiciera.

In the past, sir, young girls
didn't study or read,
nor hear those Frenchified
phrases in all their days.

. . . .

As I was saying, sir,
girls did not study then,
but they knew how to scrub
and sweep with a vengeance!

They could spin like spiders,
knead bread, sift; but I bet
they wondered if the Goths
invaded Spain or not.

Why should a woman care
who exports cacao
or if cod is a fish
as long as she can cook?

. . . .

And you, my friend, would like
a girl to raise her voice?
And I should rhyme? . . . Dearly
I'd pay for such a crime.

Las *masas* horrorizadas
pondrían al cielo el grito,
tristes frases de mi escrito
en hora aciaga trazadas.

¡¡¡Cual quedara mi persona
mordida por tanta boca!!!...
Me llamaran necia, loca,
visionaria, doctorona;

Sin amor ni compasión
algunos con tono ambiguo,
dicen que de escrito antiguo
es copia mi concepción.

Algún otro maldiciente
chilla con acre ironía:
"Es más fea que una arpía
esa niña impertinente;

Sin aseo la loquilla,
siempre a vueltas con Cervantes,
recitando consonantes
de Calderón o Zorrilla,

The horrified *masses*
would raise their raucous cries,
mocking my sad verses,
penned in a bitter hour.

What would become of me,
bad-mouthed by so many
calling me smarty-pants,
crazy, loony, dreamer?

With no love or mercy,
some would insinuate
that my compositions
are copied from a text.

And evil tongues would wag
with acrid irony:
"What an ugly harpy,
this impertinent girl!

"The unkempt little fool,
reciting Cervantes
and always quoting from
Calderón, Zorrilla;

¿Cómo podrá gobernar
bien su casa? ¡Es imposible!"
Cual si fuera incompatible
coser y raciocinar.

. . . .

¡Anatema al escribir,
al meditar y leer!
Amigo, sólo coser,
o murmurar y… dormir.

Julio de 1837

Poesías

"How can she possibly
be a good housekeeper?"
As if to stitch and think
couldn't go hand in hand.

. . . .

A curse upon writing,
meditating, reading!
My friend, only sewing,
murmuring and . . . sleeping.

July 1837

El beso maternal

(selecciones)

¿Qué valen las caricias,
los abrazos y besos
si no son prodigados
por maternal afecto?
Es la amistad efímera,
el amor pasajero,
humo fugaz la gloria,
y el porvenir incierto.
¡Ay!, sólo es positivo
el cariño materno.
¿Buscáis amistad firme,
afecto duradero,
y en el amor y gloria
un porvenir risueño?
pues bien, lo hallaréis sólo
en el materno pecho.

. . . .

Tú no puedes comprender
la dicha de poseer
lo que tienes, niño, ahora;
lo que vale esa mujer
que ríe con tu placer
y que si tú lloras, llora;

A Mother's Kiss

(excerpts)

What good are caresses,
embraces, and kisses
if they are not bestowed
with maternal fondness?
Friendship is volatile
and love temporary,
glory just fleeting smoke,
the future uncertain.
Oh, what's definite is
a mother's tenderness.
Are you seeking constant
friendship, enduring love,
and a pleasant future
filled with love and glory?
You can only find this
in a maternal heart.

. . . .

You still can't understand
the good fortune, my child,
of having what you have;
or value the woman
who laughs when you are pleased
and sheds tears when you cry;

Que vela siempre a tu lado
con solícito cuidado,
y tu querer adivina
su amor desinteresado
tan dulce, tan sosegado
como el aura matutina.

. . . .

¡Oh!, si Dios por su clemencia
mi madre me devolviera,
y bendecirme pudiera,
hija llamarme una vez!
Por verme contra su pecho
estrechada con ternura,
¡Dios mío!, por tal ventura,
¿qué no daría después?

Diera mi amor en la tierra,
belleza, si la tuviera,
mi dicha, mi vida entera
por un beso maternal;
mas que fuera el esqueleto
que de la huesa se alzara
el que tierno me besara
con su boca sepulchral.

Who watches over you
with affectionate care;
whose selfless devotion,
gentle and tranquil as
the early morning dawn,
guesses your every wish.
. . . .
Oh, merciful God, if
you'd return my mother
to bless me and call me
her daughter once again!
To find myself held tight
in her warm arms—my God,
to be so fortunate,
what wouldn't I renounce?

I'd give my earthly joy,
beauty, had I any,
happiness, my whole life,
for a maternal kiss;
but let the skeleton
who rises from the tomb
give me a tender kiss
with her sepulchral lips.

Yo sé bien que este cariño
no sería frío, inerte,
que más allá de la muerte
llevan las madres su amor;
un beso fuera de fuego
y de la gloria un destello,
ardiente, célico, bello
cual la gracia del Señor.

Octubre de 1837

Poesías

I am certain hers would
not be a cold embrace,
for mothers carry their
affection beyond death;
the kiss would be fiery,
like a spark of glory,
luminous, celestial,
just like the grace of God.

October 1837

El velo perdido

Ayer el cierzo soplaba
con impulso tan violento
que me arrebató el abrigo
con que cubriste mi seno.
    De entonces, madre,
    mala me siento.
    ¡Ay, madrecita!,
    malhaya el viento.

Yo quise desatentada
correr a su alcanzamiento;
pero Minguillo se opuso…
Galán es, madre, el mancebo.
Sobre mi desnuda espalda,
con ligero movimiento,
tendió su robusto brazo
por resguardarla del cierzo.
    De entonces, madre,
    mala me siento.
    ¡Ay, madrecita!,
    malhaya el viento.

The Lost Shawl

Yesterday the north wind
blew with such violence
that it ripped off the shawl
that you had draped on me.
    Since then, Mother,
    I feel unwell!
    Oh, dear Mother,
    cursed be the wind!

Heedlessly, I wanted
to run and retrieve it;
but Minguillo said no . . .
Mother, he's so gallant.
On my naked shoulder,
with a gentle gesture,
he placed his robust arm
as shelter from the wind.
    Since then, Mother,
    I feel unwell!
    Oh, dear Mother,
    cursed be the wind!

Yo bien dije: suelta, Mingo,
y el rostro vuelve al momento,
que madre dice pecara
el que me viera sin velo.
Mas él repuso: si peco,
en no mirarte consiento;
sírveme de lazarillo,
que ya por mi fe voy ciego.
  De entonces, madre,
  mala me siento.
  ¡Ay, madrecita!,
  malhaya el viento.

Llevó ligero su diestra
ante los ojos con tiento,
dejando sólo a sus niñas
brillar entre dedo y dedo;
Y con la izquierda en mis hombros
cual ciego de nacimiento,
por no dar traspiés pasito
llegamos aquende el pueblo.
  De entonces, madre,
  mala me siento.
  ¡Ay, madrecita!,
  malhaya el viento.

And I told him: Let go,
Mingo, and turn away,
Mother says it's sinful
to see my shoulders bared.
But he replied: If I
sin by looking at you,
then be my guide, I swear,
I am completely blind.
    Since then, Mother,
    I feel unwell!
    Oh, dear Mother,
    cursed be the wind!

Playfully he placed his
right hand over his eyes,
so only his pupils
shone between his fingers.
His left on my shoulder,
like someone blind from birth,
with small steps to avoid
stumbling, we reached the town.
    Since then, Mother,
    I feel unwell!
    Oh, dear Mother,
    cursed be the wind!

Acá cobró vista el mozo,
fue el cierzo menos violento,
y revuelto entre zarzales
hallé mi perdido velo.
   De entonces, madre,
   mala me siento.
   ¡Ay, madrecita!,
   malhaya el viento.

Marzo de 1841

Poesías

Here the lad's sight returned,
the wind blew less fiercely,
and, entangled in the
bush, I found my lost shawl.

  Since then, Mother,
  I feel unwell!
  Oh, dear Mother,
  cursed be the wind!

March 1841

Als bons pagesos i proletaris del Empordà

Ab motiu del primer concurs agrícola de Figueres

(fragmento)

Jo no sé quín encís
tenen aquexes festes
hont lo bon català
son noble instint desplega.
¿Què tenen los cantars
de ma native llengua,
que lo cor al sentirlos
bat més fort i depressa,
i sonriuen els llavis,
i los ulls s'humitejan?
¿No té armonía i gracia
la parla de Castella,
dolsura la toscana
i forsa la francesa?
Donchs, ¿per què quan els càntichs
nostres paysans axecan
ab acents d'alegría,
d'amor ò de tristesa,
totes les melodíes
olvidem de la terra,
com tota veu s'olvida
sentint la veu maternal?
¡Oh, què dols es probarne

To the Worthy Peasants and Laborers of Empordà

In Celebration of the First Agricultural Fair in Figueres

(excerpt)

What is the special charm
of those celebrations
where a good Catalan
shows his noble instincts?
Why do those melodies
in my native language
make our hearts beat faster
and stronger? Why do they
bring a smile to our lips
and fill our eyes with tears?
Doesn't Castilian have
a harmonious grace?
Isn't Italian sweet
and French full of vigor?
Why, then, upon hearing
our countrymen intone
these melodies with notes
of happiness, love, or
melancholy, do we
forget all other songs?
Why does the maternal
voice silence all others?
How sweet it is to feel

exa santa tendresa,
que als turons de la patria
ab flors ens encadena!
I quan la patria es noble,
i, com la nostra, immensa
es la gloria dels titols
de sa antigua noblesa,
no hi hà orgull més legítim
que'l que sentim per ella.
¡Lo ser català es honra!
A Deu gracies rendesca
qui la sanch catalana
sent bullir en ses venes,
i en son front honrat porta
barretina vermella.
. . . .

Antología poética

this sacred tenderness
that links us with a chain
of flowers to our soil;
and when the motherland
is grand and distinguished
with a nobility
that bears ancient titles,
the pride in our homeland
is more than justified.
To be Catalan is
an honor! God be praised
by those whose veins pulsate
with Catalonian blood
and who have the honor
to wear the red wool cap.

. . . .

Grats recorts

(fragmento)

Riu que devallas
tot dolsament
formantne xifres
d'or i d'argent,

i si t'esmaltan
los raigs brillants
del sol, t'enjoyas
de fins diamants;

de dalt les serres
dels Pirineus
vens cobrant paries
dels gels i neus,

i t'aygua pura
en abundó'
per tot escampa
rica sahó.

Per'xò, riu Segre,
fas ton camí,
sempre en mitx d'ample
florit jardí.

Fond Memories

(excerpt)

River, you amble
so serenely,
creating trails of
silver and gold;

and glazed by the bright
rays of the sun,
your jewels scintillate
like fine diamonds;

from the high peaks of
the Pyrenees,
you harvest currents
of ice and snow;

and your abundant
pristine water
floods all the fields with
a rich moisture.

Whatever your route,
River Segre,
it's always amid
garden flowers.

D'exes flors una
voldría ser
per que mon càlzer,
com encenser,

aromés pròdich
de nit y jorn
les encontrades
del teu entorn.

¡Ay! jo voldría
ser cotoliu
pera en tos marges
ferhi mon niu,

ò convertirme
en rossinyol
pera seguirte
a petit vol

d'arbres en arbres
sense parar
fins hont ab l'Ebre
caus dins del mar.
. . . .

Antología poética

I wish I were one
of those flowers
so that my chalice,
like a censer,

could be gathering,
both day and night,
all the fragrances
surrounding you.

Oh, if I could be
a turtledove,
then along your shores
I'd build my nest,

or transformed into
a nightingale,
I would follow you
for a brief flight,

from tree to tree and
not pause until
where the Ebro flows
into the sea.

. . . .

Mon derrer viatge

(fragmento)

Tinch de fer un llarch viatge
a ignotes regions estenses,
mes no sé quan de partir
serà lo temps i hora certa,
ni còm ni per hont s'hi và,
ni'l pervindre que m'hi espera.
L'equipatge ha de ser poch:
tan sols una caxa estreta;
la vestimenta, senzilla
sens joyells ni cap riquesa:
negra túnica de llana,
en lo pit una creueta,
i en mon cap un ample vel
que tot lo meu còs cobresca.
Ab exos arreus humils
forsa es que la ruta emprenga;
veig que lo moment s'atansa
sens sentir ni goig ni pena,
puix lo dexar esta vall
més que entristirme m'alegra.
. . . .

Antología poética

My Final Journey

(excerpt)

I must go on a long journey
to unknown faraway places,
but I don't know either the time
or the hour I am to depart,
nor do I know the route to take
or what the future holds for me.
My luggage will be minimal,
only a narrow wooden box,
modest garments without any
jewels or other signs of wealth;
a plain black tunic made of wool
and a small cross pinned to my chest;
on my head an ample mantle,
long enough to cloak my body.
I must embark on the journey
with these unpretentious trappings.
I see the moment drawing near,
feeling neither joy nor sorrow,
for leaving this vale fills me less
with sadness than with contentment.

. . . .

Gertrudis Gómez de Avellaneda (1814–73)

Gertrudis Gómez de Avellaneda y Arteaga
Pseudonyms: La Peregrina, Felipe Escalada,
La Golondrina, Dolores Gil de Taboada

Nicknamed Tula by her friends and referred to as La Avellaneda by Spanish critics, this poet, novelist, and dramatist is claimed by Cuba, her birth country, and Spain, where she spent most of her life. She served as president of the Sociedad Abolicionista Española ("Spanish Abolitionist Society"), and her antislavery novel *Sab* appeared in 1841, nine years before Harriet Beecher Stowe's *Uncle Tom's Cabin.* That same year, Gómez de Avellaneda published her first collection of verses, *Poesías,* which contains one of her best-known poems, "Al partir" ("Leaving"). This sonnet, often included in anthologies, expresses the speaker's feelings of nostalgia on having to leave her beloved island at the age of twenty-two.

Two other frequently anthologized poems, although very different, are both known as "A él" ("To Him"). The first poem bearing that title was written in 1840 and published in 1841; the second one, written in 1845 and published in the second edition of *Poesías* (1850), was actually called "A ***." It is generally assumed that both poems were addressed to Ignacio Cepeda, with whom Gómez de Avellaneda had a turbulent and passionate relationship. There is also some speculation that the intended recipient of the second poem may have been the poet Gabriel García Tassara, who never acknowledged the paternity of her daughter. In contrast to the early "A él," which refers to the beloved with mystic imagery and diction reminiscent of Santa Teresa, the later one expresses disenchantment and rejection.

Al partir

¡Perla del mar! ¡Estrella de occidente!
¡Hermosa Cuba! tu brillante cielo
la noche cubre con su opaco velo
como cubre el dolor mi triste frente.

¡Voy a partir!... La chusma diligente
para arrancarme del nativo suelo
las velas iza y pronta a su desvelo
la brisa acude de tu zona ardiente.

¡Adiós, patria feliz, edén querido!
¡Doquier que el hado en su furor me impela,
tu dulce nombre halagará mi oído!

¡Adiós!... ¡Ya cruje la turgente vela...
el ancla se alza,... el buque, estremecido,
las olas corta y silencioso vuela!

Abril de 1836

Poesías (1850)

Leaving

Pearl of the sea! Star of the West!
Lovely Cuba! With its dark veil
the night covers your brilliant sky
as pain covers my sad forehead.

I am leaving! . . . The busy crew
hoists the sails that are to tear me
away from my native soil, and
swiftly the hot breeze extends them.

Farewell, happy land, my Eden!
Where'er furious fate destines
me, your sweet name will please my ear!

Farewell! . . . the puffed-up sails creak now . . .
anchor lifted . . . the jolted boat
cuts the waves and flies silently!

April 1836

Imitación de Petrarca

No encuentro paz, ni me conceden guerra;
de fuego devorado, siento el frío;
abrazo al mundo, y quédome vacío;
me lanzo al cielo, y préndeme la tierra.

Ni libre soy, ni la prisión me encierra;
veo sin luz, sin voz hablar ansío;
temo sin esperar, sin placer río;
nada me da valor, nada me aterra.

Busco el peligro cuando auxilio imploro;
al sentirme morir me encuentro fuerte;
valiente pienso ser, y débil lloro.

Cúmplese así mi extraordinaria suerte;
siempre a los pies de la beldad que adoro,
y no quiere mi vida, ni mi muerte.

Diciembre de 1836

Poesías (1850)

In Imitation of Petrarch

I find no peace but cannot wage war;
though consumed by fire, I suffer cold;
I embrace the world but feel alone;
I reach for the sky, but earth binds me.

I am not free, nor do walls hold me;
I see without light, speak without voice;
I fear without hope, laugh without joy;
nothing emboldens or frightens me.

I look for danger but call for help;
feeling my life wane makes me stronger;
I long to be brave yet cry meekly.

This is how my strange fate is fulfilled:
at the feet of my beloved beauty
who wants neither my life nor my death.

December 1836

A las estrellas

Reina el silencio: fúlgidas en tanto,
luces de paz, purísimas estrellas,
de la noche feliz lámparas bellas,
bordáis con oro su luctuoso manto.

Duerme el placer, mas vela mi quebranto,
y rompen el silencio mis querellas,
volviendo el eco, unísono con ellas,
de aves nocturnas el siniestro canto.

¡Estrellas, cuya luz modesta y pura
del mar duplica el azulado espejo!
Si a compasión os mueve la amargura
del intenso penar por que me quejo,
¿cómo para aclarar mi noche oscura
no tenéis, ¡ay!, ni un pálido reflejo?

Septiembre de 1837

Poesías (1850)

To the Stars

Silence reigns, while you, resplendent
lights of peace, pure stars, beautiful
and cheerful lamps of the night, stitch
her sorrowful mantle with gold.

Pleasure sleeps; my pain keeps vigil
and my laments break the silence,
their echo joining that of the
nocturnal birds' sinister song.

Stars, you whose modest and pure light
reflects in the sea's blue mirror!
If you feel compassion for the
bitterness of my intense pain,
why do you not light my dark night
with even a pale reflection?

September 1837

A una mariposa

Fugaz mariposa,
que de oro y zafir
las alas ostentas,
alegre y feliz.

¡Cuál siguen mis ojos
tu vuelo gentil,
que al soplo despliegas
del aura de abril!

Ya rauda te lanzas
al bello jardín,
ya en rápidos giros
te acercas a mí.

Del sol a los rayos
que empieza a lucir
¡con cuánta riqueza
te brinda el pensil!

Sus flores la acacia
despliega por ti
y el clavel fragrante
su ardiente rubí.

To a Butterfly

Swift butterfly, you
display your sapphire
and gold-colored wings
with delight and joy.

How my eyes follow
your graceful flight as
you flutter on the
breath of April's breeze!

At times you dash to
the lovely garden
or you circle me,
swirling rapidly.

And with the rays of
the first morning sun,
the flowers welcome
you with, oh, such wealth!

The acacia yields
its blossoms to you,
and the carnation,
its ardent scarlet.

Abre la violeta
su seno turquí,
la anemone luce
su vario matiz.

Ya libas el lirio,
ya el fresco alhelí,
ya trémula besas
el blanco jazmín.

Mas ¡ay!, ¡cuán en vano
mil flores y mil
por fijar se afanan
tu vuelo sin fin! …

¡Ay!, que ya te lleva
tu audaz frenesí,
do ostenta la rosa
su puro carmín.

¡Temeraria, tente!
¿Dó vas, infeliz?…
¿No ves las espinas
de punto sutil?

The violet reveals
its turquoise foliage;
the anemone
glows with varied tints.

From the iris or
the prim wallflower,
you drink, and trembling
kiss the white jasmine.

But, oh, how many
thousands of flowers
try in vain to halt
your unbounded flight!

Oh, how soon your bold
frenzy leads you where
the rose displays her
faultless crimson hues!

Stop, foolhardy one!
Where are you going?
Don't you see the thorns
with their subtle barbs?

¡Torna a tu violeta!
¡Torna a tu alhelí!
No quieras, incauta,
clavada morir.

Abril de 1838

Poesías (1850)

Go to your violet!
And your wallflower!
Turn back or you risk
being pierced to death.

April 1838

A él

(fragmento)

Era la edad lisonjera
en que es un sueño la vida,
era la aurora hechicera
de mi juventud florida
en su sonrisa primera

cuando sin rumbo vagaba
por el campo, silenciosa,
y en escuchar me gozaba
la tórtola que entonaba
su querella lastimosa.

Melancólico fulgor
blanca luna repartía,
y el aura leve mecía
con soplo murmurador
la tierna flor que se abría.

¡Y yo gozaba! El rocío,
nocturno llanto del cielo,
el bosque espeso y umbrío,
la dulce quietud del suelo,
el manso correr del río,

To Him

(excerpt)

It was that lovely time
when all life seemed a dream,
it was the charming dawn
of my youth blossoming
with its very first smile,

when I roamed the meadows
aimlessly, in silence,
listening blissfully
to the turtledove coo
its heartrending lament.

The pale white moon cast a
melancholy shimmer,
and with murmuring breath
the light wind gently rocked
the fragile waking bud.

And I rejoiced! The dew—
the sky's nocturnal tears—
the forest, dense and dark,
the earth's sweet peacefulness,
the river's tranquil flow,

y de la luna el albor,
y el aura que murmuraba
acariciando a la flor,
y el pájaro que cantaba...
todo me hablaba de amor.

Y trémula, palpitante,
en mi delirio extasiada,
miré una visión brillante,
como el aire perfumada
como las nubes flotante.

Ante mí resplandecía
como un astro brillador,
y mi loca fantasía
al fantasma seductor
tributaba idolatría.

Escuchar pensé su acento
en el canto de las aves;
eran las auras su aliento
cargadas de aromas suaves,
y su estancia el firmamento.

¿Qué ser extraño era aquél?
¿Era un ángel o era un hombre?

and the pale white moonlight,
and the murmuring breeze
caressing the flower,
the singing of the bird . . .
all spoke to me of love.

Tremulous, quivering,
delirious with bliss,
I beheld a brilliant
vision, perfumed like air
and floating like the clouds.

Like a luminous star
it shone before me and
my wild fantasy paid
idolatrous tribute
to the seductive ghost.

I seemed to hear his voice
in the songs the birds sang;
the breezes were his breath
filled with sweet fragrances,
the heavens his abode.

What strange being was this?
Was it angel or man?

¿Era un Dios o era Luzbel?

¿Mi visión no tiene nombre?

¡Ah! nombre tiene… ¡Era *Él!*

. . . .

Noviembre de 1840

Poesías (1850)

Was it God or Satan?

Has my vision no name?

Oh, it has a name . . . *He!*

. . . .

November 1840

Mi mal

A...

En vano ansiosa tu amistad procura
adivinar el mal que me atormenta;
en vano, amigo, conmovida intenta
revelarlo mi voz a tu ternura.

Puede explicarse el ansia, la locura
con que el amor sus fuegos alimenta...
Puede el dolor, la saña más violenta,
exhalar por el labio su amargura...

Mas de decir mi malestar profundo,
no halla mi voz, mi pensamiento, medio,
y al indagar su origen me confundo:

pero es un mal terrible, sin remedio,
que hace odiosa la vida, odioso el mundo,
que seca el corazón... ¡En fin, es tedio!

Noviembre de 1841

Poesías (1850)

My Torment

To . . .

In vain, your friendship has made you anxious
to determine what torment afflicts me;
in vain, my friend, touched by your tenderness,
my voice has tried to reveal it to you.

Anxiousness and the madness fueled by
the fiery flames of love can be explained . . .
Lips can exhale the bitterness of woes
as well as of most malicious fury . . .

But my voice and thoughts have no medium
to express my profound uneasiness,
and searching for its cause leaves me confused:

it is an awful torment without cure,
that makes both life and world so odious
and drains the heart . . . In short, it's tedium!

November 1841

Soneto imitando una oda de Safo

¡Feliz quien junto a ti por ti suspira!
¡Quien oye el eco de tu voz sonora!
¡Quien el halago de tu risa adora
y el blando aroma de tu aliento aspira!

Ventura tanta—que envidiosa admira
el querubín que en el empíreo mora—
el alma turba, al corazón devora,
y el torpe acento, al expresarla, expira.

Ante mis ojos desparece el mundo,
y por mis venas circular ligero
el fuego siento del amor profundo.

Trémula, en vano resistirte quiero...
de ardiente llanto mi mejilla inundo,
¡deliro, gozo, te bendigo y muero!

Julio de 1842
Poesías (1850)

Sonnet in Imitation of an Ode by Sappho

Happy the one who near you pines for you!
Who hears the echo of your vibrant voice!
Who adores the caress of your smile and
inhales the soothing fragrance of your breath!

Such good fortune—admired and envied
by cherubs in their celestial abode—
unsettles the soul, overwhelms the heart,
and the inept voice fails to express it.

The world disappears before my eyes as
I endure the fire of a profound love
that pulsates weightlessly throughout my veins.

Trembling, I try to resist you in vain . . .
passionate tears flood down upon my cheeks
with rapture and joy, I bless you and die!

July 1842

El recuerdo importuno

¿Serás del alma eterna compañera,
tenaz memoria de veloz ventura?...
¿Por qué el recuerdo interminable dura,
si el bien pasó cual ráfaga ligera?

¡Tú, negro olvido, que con hambre fiera
abres ¡ay! sin cesar tu boca oscura,
de glorias mil inmensa sepultura
y del dolor consolación postrera!

Si a tu vasto poder ninguno asombra,
y al orbe riges con tu cetro frío,
¡ven! que su Dios mi corazón te nombra.

¡Ven y devora este fantasma impío,
de pasado placer pálida sombra,
de placer por venir nublo sombrío!

Abril de 1843

Poesías (1850)

Unwelcome Remembrance

Are you the soul's eternal companion,
tenacious memory of fleeting bliss . . . ?
Why does remembrance persist forever
when good times pass like a swift gust of wind?

Black oblivion, you never cease to
open your dark jaws like a hungry beast;
you are the huge tomb of a thousand joys
and suffering's final consolation.

If none overshadows your vast power
and you rule the world with your cold scepter,
come, for my heart will declare you its god.

Come and devour this irreverent ghost,
this pallid shadow of bygone pleasures,
this somber cloud over pleasures yet to come.

April 1843

A la luna

Imitación de Byron

¡Sol del que triste vela!
¡Astro de lumbre fría
cuyos trémulos rayos, de la noche
para mostrar las sombras sólo brillan!

¡Oh, cuánto te semejas
de la pasada dicha
al pálido recuerdo, que del alma
sólo hace ver la soledad sombría!

Luz de pasados tiempos
ya lánguida y marchita,
vive en la mente, pero no la enciende;
luce en secreto, pero no ilumina.

Descubre, cual tú, sombras
que esmalta y acaricia;
y como a ti, tan sólo la contempla
el dolor mudo en férvida vigilia.

Mayo de 1843

Poesías (1850)

To the Moon

In imitation of Byron

Sun of the sleepless!
Star of icy light
whose quivering rays sparkle only
to reflect the shadows of the night!

Oh, you resemble
that pale memory
of past happiness that exposes
the somber solitude of the soul!

A light of times past,
now weak and wilted,
it lives in the mind but gives no warmth,
it shines faintly but does not illume.

It too finds shadows
to touch and caress;
and mute sorrow, in fervent vigil,
merely contemplates that light and you.

May 1843

Al destino

Escrito estaba, sí: se rompe en vano
una vez y otra la fatal cadena,
y mi vigor por recobrar me afano.
Escrito estaba: el cielo me condena
a tornar siempre al cautiverio rudo,
    y yo obediente acudo
    restaurando eslabones
que cada vez más rigidos me oprimen;
pues del yugo fatal no me redimen
de mi altivez postreras convulsiones.

¡Heme aquí! ¡Tuya soy! ¡Dispón, destino,
de tu víctima dócil! Yo me entrego
cual la hoja seca al raudo torbellino
    que la arrebata ciego.
¡Tuya soy! ¡Heme aquí! ¡Todo lo puedes!
Tu capricho es mi ley: sacia tu saña...
Pero sabe, ¡oh cruel!, que no me engaña
la sonrisa falaz que hoy me concedes.

Junio de 1844
Poesías (1850)

To Destiny

Written it was, yes: time and time again
the fatal chain is broken in vain, and
I strive to recover my energy.
Written it was: heaven has condemned me
to return to a harsh captivity,
and I accept obediently,
repairing the broken links that
oppress me with increased rigidity;
for not even the last spasms of my
pride can redeem me from the fatal yoke.

Here I am! I am yours! Do as you please,
destiny, I am your docile victim!
I surrender like a dry leaf to the
blind and whipping winds of a storm
I am yours! Here I am! Do as you wish!
Your whim is my law! Satisfy your rage . . .
But know, O cruel one, that I am not
fooled by the false smile you grant me today.

June 1844

A ***

No existe lazo ya: todo está roto:
Plúgole al cielo así: ¡bendito sea!
Amargo cáliz con placer agoto:
Mi alma reposa al fin: nada desea.

Te amé, no te amo ya: piénsolo al menos;
¡Nunca, si fuere error, la verdad mire!
Que tantos años de amarguras llenos
trague el olvido; el corazón respire.

Lo has destrozado sin piedad: mi orgullo
una vez y otra vez pisaste insano:
mas nunca el labio exhalará un murmullo
para acusar tu proceder tirano.

De grandes faltas vengador terrible,
dócil llenaste tu misión: ¿lo ignoras?
No era tuyo el poder que irresistible
postró ante ti mis fuerzas vencedoras.

Quísolo Dios y fue: ¡gloria a su nombre!
Todo se terminó: recobro aliento:
¡Ángel de las venganzas!, ya eres hombre…
Ni amor ni miedo al contemplarte siento.

To ***

The knot's undone; all ties severed.
Heaven has willed it so: Praise be!
I down the bitter drink with joy;
my soul rests; I have no desire.

I loved you, but no more, I think;
if I erred, spare me from the truth!
May these acrid years be swallowed
by oblivion; my heart breathes.

You have destroyed it without pity;
trampled my pride repeatedly . . .
But no accusation about
your tyranny will cross my lips.

Avenger of terrible faults,
you meekly fulfilled your mission.
Didn't you know? The power that
subdued my forces was not yours.

God willed it: glory to His name!
All is finished; I breathe again.
Angel of vengeance, now merely
a man I neither love nor fear.

Cayó tu cetro, se embotó tu espada…
Mas, ¡ay!, ¡cuán triste libertad respiro!
Hice un mundo de ti, que hoy se anonada,
y en honda y vasta soledad me miro.

¡Vive dichoso tú! Si en algún día
ves este *adiós* que te dirijo eterno,
sabe que aún tienes en el alma mía,
generoso perdón, cariño tierno.

Noviembre de 1845

Poesías (1850)

Your scepter fell, your sword is blunt . . .
But, oh, how sad my liberty!
You were my world, and it collapsed—
my solitude cuts broad and deep.

Live in happiness! If one day
you should read this final adieu,
you'll see in my soul generous
pardon and tender affection.

November 1845

Significado de la palabra *yo amé*

Imitación de Parny

Con "*yo amé*" dice cualquiera
esta verdad desolante:
—Todo en el mundo es quimera,
no hay ventura verdadera
ni sentimiento constante.—

Yo amé significa: —Nada
le basta al hombre jamás;
la pasión más delicada,
la promesa más sagrada,
son humo y viento… y no más!

Diciembre de 1845

Poesías (1850)

The Meaning of the Words *I Loved*

In imitation of Parny

Whoever says *I loved*
conveys this painful truth:
"In this world all is sham;
there is no true bliss or
feelings of faithfulness."

I loved means: "Nothing is
quite enough for mankind:
the most delicate passion
and the holiest vow
are smoke and wind . . . no more!"

December 1845

Romance

No soy *maga* ni *sirena*,
ni *querub* ni *pitonisa*,
como en tus versos galanos
me llamas hoy, bella niña.

Gertrudis tengo por nombre,
cual recibido en la pila;
me dice *Tula* mi madre,
y mis amigos la imitan.

Prescinde, pues, te lo ruego,
de las *Safos* y *Corinas*,
y simplemente me nombra
Gertrudis, *Tula* o amiga.

Amiga, sí; aunque tanto
contra tu sexo te indignas,
y de maligno lo acusas
y de envidioso lo tildas.

En mí pretendo probarte
que hay en almas femeninas,
para lo hermoso entusiasmo,
para lo bueno justicia.

Ballad

I am no *wizard* or *siren*,
neither *cherub* nor *sorceress,*
as you refer to me in your
chivalrous poem, my lovely girl.

Gertrudis is the name I bear,
given to me in baptism;
my mother calls me *Tula* and,
just like her, my friends do the same.

So, I beg you not to give me
names such as *Sappho* or *Corinne*,
and simply refer to me as
Gertrudis, *Tula*, or as friend.

Friend, yes, for though you manifest
such disdain toward your gender,
accusing it of malice and
denouncing it as envious,

I hope to serve as proof to you
that the feminine soul contains
enthusiasm for beauty,
a sense of justice for the good.

Naturaleza madrastra
no fue (lo ves en ti misma)
con la mitad de la especie
que la razón ilumina.

No son las fuerzas corpóreas
de las del alma medida;
no se encumbra el pensamiento
por el vigor de las fibras.

Perdona, pues, si no acato
aquel fallo que me intimas;
como no acepto el elogio
en que lo envuelves benigna.

No, no aliento ambición noble,
como engañada imaginas,
de que en páginas de gloria
mi humilde nombre se escriba.

Canto como canta el ave.
como las ramas se agitan,
como las fuents murmuran,
como las auras suspiran.

Canto porque al cielo plugo
darme el estro que me anima;

Nature was not a stepmother—
as you can well see in yourself—
with that half of humanity
that reason has well enlightened.

Physical strength does not imply
that the soul is equally strong
and thought does not soar loftily
because of powerful sinews.

So forgive me if I do not
acknowledge the fault you suggest;
just as I do not agree with
the kind praise you bestow on me.

I have no noble ambition—
as you mistakenly believe—
to see my humble name written
on the great pages of glory.

I sing just as the birds must sing,
just as the tree branches must sway,
just as the fountains must murmur,
just as the soft breezes must sigh.

I sing, for it pleased heaven to
provide me with inspiration,

como dio brillo a los astros,
como dio al orbe armonías.

Canto porque hay en mi pecho
secretas cuerdas que vibran
a cada afecto del alma,
a cada azar de la vida.

Canto porque hay luz y sombras,
porque hay pesar y alegría,
porque hay temor y esperanza,
porque hay amor y hay perfidía.

Canto porque existo y siento,
porque lo grande me admira,
porque lo bello me encanta,
porque lo malo me irrita.

Canto porque ve mi mente
concordancias infinitas,
y placers misteriosos,
y verdades escondidas.

Canto porque hay en los seres
sus condiciones precisas:
corre el agua, vuela el ave,
silba el viento, y el sol brilla.

as it gave the stars their brilliance
and gave harmony to the spheres.

I sing, for in my breast there are
secret chords that resonate with
every sentiment the soul feels
and with life's every vagary.

I sing, for there is light and shade,
there is mourning and ecstasy,
there is apprehension and hope,
there is passion and betrayal.

I sing, for I exist and feel,
for majesty impresses me,
for loveliness fascinates me,
for wickedness irritates me.

I sing because my mind perceives
innumerable concordances,
and pleasures filled with mystery
and truths that lie hidden from view.

I sing because all human beings
have an essential condition;
waters must flow and birds must fly,
the wind whistles and the sun shines.

Canto sin saber yo propia
lo que el canto significa,
y si al mundo, que lo escucha,
asombro o lástima inspira.

El ruiseñor no ambiciona
que lo aplaudan cuando trina,
latidos son de su seno
sus nocturnas melodías.

Modera, pues, tu alabanza,
y de mi frente retira
la inmarchitable corona
que tu amor me pronostica.

Premiando nobles esfuerzos,
sienes más heroicas ciña;
que yo al cantar sólo cumplo
la condición de mi vida.

Enero de 1846
Poesías (1850)

I sing without understanding
the exact meaning of my song,
and whether, upon hearing it,
the world feels alarm or pity.

The nightingale does not aspire
to be applauded when he trills;
his nocturnal melodies are
merely the heartbeats in his breast.

So moderate your eulogy
and take away from my forehead
the imperishable wreath that
your love foresees as meant for me.

Encircle more heroic brows
in honor of their noble feats,
for by singing I do no more
than fulfill my life's destiny.

January 1846

Concepción Arenal
(1820–93)
Concepción Arenal de García Carrasco

Born in El Ferrol (Galicia), the noted Spanish poet, sociologist, penologist, and staunch feminist was an energetic force behind reform in education and the penal system. Since women were barred from studying at the university, Concepción Arenal attended law classes dressed in men's clothing. Her writings on political, sociological, and philosophical subjects were influential and translated into several languages. The two fables featured here illustrate her didactic bent and are taken from her *Fábulas en verso originales* ("Original Fables in Verse"), a book that was used as a text in Spanish grade schools. "La esclavitud de los negros" ("The Slavery of Blacks"), an impassioned argument against slavery on moral and religious grounds, won first prize in the poetry contest sponsored by the Spanish Abolitionist Society. The society's *Cancionero del esclavo* ("A Slave's Songbook"), published in 1866 with a selection of the best contest entries, included Arenal's ode in its entirety (494 lines).

XXVIII: El hierro y el topacio

"¿Por qué tan preciso al mundo
—dijo el hierro amostazado—,
soy menos que tú pagado?
¡de pensarlo me confundo!
Ni cabaña ni palacio
existir puede sin mí;
¿tú para que sirves, di?"
Y le respondió el topacio:
"Una sencilla verdad
te dará la explicación:
tú sirves a la razón,
yo sirvo a la vanidad.
Fijos dos hechos verás
aunque de justicia ajenos:
que la razón paga menos,
la vanidad paga más".

Fábulas

XXVIII: Iron and Topaz

"If the world needs me, why,"
said Iron with annoyance,
"am I paid less than you?
That's what confuses me!
No cabin or palace
can exist without me;
what use are you, pray tell?"
To which Topaz replied,
"The explanation is
found in this simple truth:
you are reason's servant,
while I serve vanity.
Recognize these two facts—
unjust though they be—
reason pays a pittance,
vanity pays much more."

XLII: La rosa y la espina

Fresca, olorosa, lozana,
de tentarle muy capaz,
cogió una rosa un rapaz
de mayo cierta mañana.
El triste no imaginó
que, en objeto así precioso,
nada hubiera de dañoso,
y una espina se clavó.
"Padre, ¿a qué tanta belleza?
si hace daño, ¿a qué ese olor?"
"Hijo, el placer y el dolor
mezcló la nauraleza.
Misterio, en verdad, profundo,
pero, como en el rosal,
mezclados el bien y el mal
has de encontrar en el mundo."

Fábulas

XLII: The Rose and the Thorn

Fresh, fragrant, full-blossomed,
with a tempting allure,
was the rose the lad plucked
one fine morning in May.
Sadly unsuspecting
that such a precious thing
could cause any harm, he
pierced himself with a thorn.
"Father, why such beauty
and sweet smell if it hurts?"
"My son, Nature combines
pleasure with suffering.
It's a deep mystery
but, as in the rosebush,
so in the world, you'll find
evil entwined with good."

La esclavitud de los negros

(fragmento)

¡Esclavitud! ¿Cómo este horrible nombre,
que es opresión, iniquidades, llanto,
fuerza brutal, depravación, espanto,
puede el hombre escuchar? ¡Qué digo el hombre!
Dijérase que aterra,
que inspira el horror mismo,
en el mar proceloso, en la ancha tierra,
de la región del sol, hasta el abismo.
El rugir del león ensangrentado;
la tórtola, arrullando con voz tierna,
la estéril roca, el valle dilatado,
el ardiente volcán, la nieve eterna,
las aves que nos cantan sus amores,
el sauce que en las aguas se reclina,
el torrente que estrago en pos derrama,
fecundador el caudaloso río,
la escarcha y el rocío,
la fuente que murmura, el mar que brama,
la garza que hasta el cielo se levanta,
la fiera que su presa descuartiza,
todo le dice al hombre que esclaviza,
"¡Sacrílego! ¡Has hollado la ley santa!"
. . . .

El cancionero

The Slavery of Blacks

(excerpt)

Slavery! How can humanity
bear to hear this awful name: brute force,
oppression, evil, vice, tears, and fear?
Did I say humanity? It seems
to horrify
and fill with dread
the stormy sea, the entire earth,
from sun-capped peaks to the abyss.
The roar of the blood-covered lion,
the turtledove, cooing tenderly,
the barren rock, the sweeping valley,
burning volcanoes, eternal snow,
birds singing to us about their loves,
the willow bending into the stream,
the ravages in the torrent's wake,
the river brimming with fruitfulness,
hoarfrost and dew,
the brook that murmurs, the roaring sea,
the heron rising to the heavens,
the beast tearing to pieces its prey,
everything tells the man who enslaves,
"Profaner! You've defiled sacred law!"

Carolina Coronado
(1820–1911)
Carolina Coronado y Romero
Carolina Coronado de Perry

The collection of thirty-seven poems, *Poesías* (1843), by Carolina Coronado, appeared only two years after the publication of similarly titled books by María Josepa Massanés and Gertrudis Gómez de Avellaneda. In addition to the nearly five hundred poems Coronado wrote during her long life, she authored plays, novels, and articles. She praised, encouraged, and actively supported the writings of other women and played a key role in a circle of feminine poets who, in need of mutual support, banded together into what modern critics have dubbed the Lyrical Sisterhood.

Coronado was especially fond of Emilio, the youngest of her seven siblings, and some of her poems are addressed to him. To Alberto, the mysterious love of her life, who seems to have perished at sea, Coronado devoted a series of poems that constitutes the most sustained cycle of love poems written by a nineteenth-century woman poet. In 1852, she married Horatio J. Perry, an American diplomat, and in 1873 the couple moved to Portugal, where they spent the rest of their lives.

Like many of her contemporaries, Coronado was inspired by the widely circulated nineteenth-century legend of Sappho's unrequited love for Phaon, a young fisherman. In her sonnet "El salto de Leucades" ("Leucadia"), Coronado describes the moment that Sappho, in despair over being spurned, plunges to her death from the Leucadian rocks. In "Gloria de las flores" ("Glory of the Flowers"), Coronado compares her poems to flowers and worries about whether they are also fated to wilt and be forgotten. In marked contrast to the predominantly lyric motifs in her poetry and that of most feminine poets, her "El marido verdugo" ("The Brutal Husband") describes, in shockingly graphic terms, the physical harm inflicted on women by violent spousal abuse.

A una gota de rocío

Lágrima viva de la fresca aurora,
a quien la mustia flor la vida debe,
y el prado ansioso entre el follaje embebe;
gota que el sol con sus reflejos dora,

que en la tez de las flores seductora
mecida por el céfiro más leve,
mezclas de grana tu color de nieve
y de nieve su grana encantadora,

ven a mezclarte con mi triste lloro,
y a consumirte en mi mejilla ardiente;
que acaso correrán más dulcemente

las lágrimas amargas que devoro...
mas ¡qué fuera una gota de rocío
perdida entre el raudal del llanto mío!...

Poesías (1852)

To a Dewdrop

Living teardrop of the new morn,
you give the wilted flower life
and quench the thirst of anxious fields;
dewdrop, gilded with the sun's rays,

you sway with the most gentle breeze,
from the flowers' seductive hue
you blend scarlet into your white,
and white into their charming red.

Come and mingle with my sad cry
and comfort my burning cheek, so
that the bitter tears I swallow

may flow along a sweeter path—
oh, what is a single dewdrop
lost within the flood of my tears!

El pájaro perdido

¡Huyó con vuelo incierto
y de mis ojos ha desparecido!...
   ¡Mirad si a vuestro huerto
   mi pájaro querido,
niñas hermosas, por acaso ha huido!

Sus ojos relucientes
son como los del águila orgullosa;
   plumas resplandecientes
   en la cabeza airosa
lleva, y su voz es tierna y armoniosa.

Mirad si cuidadoso
junto a las flores se escondió en la grama;
   ese laurel frondoso
   mirad rama por rama,
que él los laureles y las flores ama.

Si le halláis por ventura,
no os enamore su amoroso acento;
   no os prende su hermosura:
   volvédmele al momento,
o dejadle, si no, libre en el viento.

The Lost Bird

He fled from my sight,
flying away with unsteady wings!
  Lovely girls, see if
  my belovèd bird
perchance has landed in your garden.

His eyes scintillate,
like those of the majestic eagle;
  bright feathers adorn
  his elegant head;
tender is his melodious voice.

See if he's hiding
coyly near the flowers in the grass;
  search every branch of
  the luxuriant
oleander, whose bloom he adores.

If you should find him,
do not fall prey to his charming song
  or his handsome looks;
  send him back at once,
otherwise set him free in the wind.

Porque su pico de oro
sólo en mi mano toma la semilla,
    y no enjugaré el lloro
    que veis en mi mejilla
hasta encontrar mi prófuga avecilla.

Mi vista se oscurece
si sus ojos no ve, que son mi día;
    mi ánima desfallece
    con la melancolía
de no escucharle ya su melodía.

Poesías (1852)

For his golden beak
will peck the seed only from my hand,
    and the tears you see
    will flow ceaselessly
'til I find my errant little bird.

My vision darkens
if his eyes fail to brighten my day;
    my spirit grows faint
    from melancholy
if I cease to hear his melody.

El marido verdugo

¿Teméis de esa que puebla las montañas
turba de brutos fiera el desenfreno?
¡Más feroces dañinas alimañas
la madre sociedad nutre en su seno!

Bullen, de humanas formas revestidos,
torpes vivientes entre humanos seres,
que ceban el placer de sus sentidos
en el llanto infeliz de las mujeres.

No allá a las lides de su patria fueron
a exhalar de su ardor la inmensa llama;
nunca enemiga lanza acometieron;
que otra es la lid que su valor inflama.

Nunca el verdugo de inocente esposa
con noble lauro coronó su frente:
¡Ella os dirá temblando y congojosa
las gloriosas hazañas del valiente!

Ella os dirá que a veces siente el cuello
por sus manos de bronce atarazado,
y a veces el finísimo cabello
por las garras del héroe arrebatado.

The Brutal Husband

Do you fear the wanton fury
of uncultured mountain brutes?
Much fiercer are the harmful beasts
suckled at society's breast!

Taking on human form, these rude
beings swarm, mingling with mankind,
feeding their sensual pleasures
with desolate women's laments.

The flame of their valor is not
extinguished on the battlefield
or by the lance of enemies,
for a different fight inflames them.

The oppressor of a blameless wife
does not wear a wreath of laurels—
she will tell you with fear and dread
about her hero's splendid feats.

She will tell you of the many
times his bronze hands have clawed her throat
and of the times his heroic
clutches pulled her delicate hair;

Que a veces sobre el seno trasparente
cárdenas huellas de sus dedos halla;
que a veces brotan de su blanca frente
sangre las venas que su esposo estalla.

Y que ¡ay! del tierno corazón llagado
más sangre, más dolor la herida brota,
que el delicado seno macerado,
y que la vena de sus sienes rota.

Así hermosura y juventud al lado
pierde de su verdugo; así envejece:
así lirio suave y delicado
junto al áspero cardo arraiga y crece.

Y así en humanas formas escondidos,
cual bajo el agua del arroyo el cieno,
torpes vivientes al amor uncidos
la madre sociedad nutre en su seno.

Poesías (1852)

of the times his fingers have left
their purple marks on her pure breast;
and that the blood that stains her brow
flowed from the vein her husband burst.

Oh, from her fragile broken heart,
more blood and pain spring in anguish
than from her tender, abused breast
or from her forehead's shattered vein.

Thus she ages, losing both youth
and beauty at her tyrant's side;
a soft and delicate lily
entangled with the rough thistle.

Hidden behind a human form
like muck beneath the flowing brook,
rude beings who enslave with love
are suckled at society's breast.

El salto de Leucades

El sol a la mitad de su carrera
rueda entre rojas nubes escondido;
contra las rocas la oleada fiera
rompe el Leucadio mar embravecido.

Safo aparece en la escarpada orilla,
triste corona funeral ciñendo:
fuego en sus ojos sobrehumano brilla,
el asombroso espacio audaz midiendo.

Los brazos tiende, en lúgubre gemido
misteriosas palabras murmurando;
y el cuerpo de las rocas desprendido
"Faón" dice, a los aires entregando.

Giró un punto en el éter vacilante;
luego en las aguas se desploma y hunde;
el eco entre las olas fluctuante
el sonido tristísimo difunde.

Poesías (1852)

Leucadia

Midway in its heavenly path,
the sun hides behind crimson clouds;
the enraged sea breaks its fierce waves
on the rocks of Leucadia.

Crowned with a gloomy funeral wreath,
Sappho comes to the craggy shore:
boldly measuring the vast space,
an eerie fire glows in her eyes.

With a plaintive wail and outspread
arms, she murmurs mystical words;
"Phaon," she says, surrendering
her falling body to the winds.

She wavers briefly in the air,
drops into the water and sinks;
the echo, weaving in and out
of the waves, carries the sad sound.

La rosa blanca

¿Cuál de las hijas del verano ardiente,
cándida rosa, iguala a tu hermosura,
la suavísima tez y la frescura
que brotan de tu faz resplandeciente?

La sonrosada luz de alba naciente
no muestra al desplegarse más dulzura,
ni el ala de los cisnes la blancura
que el peregrino cerco de tu frente.

Así, gloria del huerto, en el pomposo
ramo descuellas desde verde asiento;
cuando llevado sobre el manso viento

a tu argentino cáliz oloroso
roba su aroma insecto licencioso,
y el puro esmalte empaña con su aliento.

Poesías (1852)

The White Rose

Which daughter of burning summer,
white rose, can equal your beauty,
delicate skin, and the youthful
blossoming of your radiant face?

Dawn's first rosy glow does not show
greater sweetness as it unfolds,
nor is the swan's wing as white as
the wondrous halo of your brow.

Garden glory, your majestic
bouquet stands out against the green;
when carried by the gentle breeze,

a rakish insect robs the scent
of your fragrant silver chalice,
and clouds its pure glow with his breath

A una coqueta

Como aquellas lucecillas
vaporosas y ligeras
que sin calor a millares
se levantan de la tierra,
los amores en tu pecho,
fragilísima belleza,
sin que su fuego te abrase
alzan mil llamas diversas:
brotan, lucen, se disipan,
otras nacen tras aquéllas;
la inconstancia las apaga,
la liviandad las renueva.

Poesías (1852)

To a Coquette

Like legions of lights,
vaporous, weightless,
that float over land
but provide no heat,
the loves in your heart,
delicate beauty,
burn with endless flames,
leaving you unscathed;
they bloom, shine, disperse;
and then glow anew—
dimmed by fickleness,
relit by caprice.

Canción [1]

Cuando la luz de la tarde
en occidente se apaga,
y la reina de las sombras
con ligero paso avanza;

en esas horas tranquilas,
inspiradoras del alma,
cuando en las alas del viento
el silencio se derrama;

cuando la tórtola dulce
lánguido suspiro exhala
con acento lastimero
recogida entre las ramas,

a aliviar voy mis cuidados
a la orilla solitaria
de un pacífico arroyuelo,
que entre fresnos se dilata.

Y vagando pensativa
por la arboleda callada,
sueño dichas venideras,
o canto las ya pasadas.

Song [1]

When the evening light
dies down in the west,
the queen of shadows
advances lithely.

In those quiet hours
that inspire the soul,
when silence splashes
the wings of the wind,

when the turtledove,
secluded amid
branches, coos sadly
with languorous sighs,

I appease my woes
on the lonely shore
of a peaceful stream,
flowing near ash trees.

Absorbed, I wander
in the soundless wood,
dreaming of future
bliss and joys long gone.

Y comparo al manso río
mi existencia sosegada.—
El rueda, blando entre flores:
ella entre ilusiones blanda.

Poesía. (1852)

Like the calm river
is my tranquil life—
flowers cushion its
course, illusions mine.

Canción [2]

Con el otoño perdidas
son las claras y lucidas
    alboradas
y las flores del estío
yacen en el valle umbrío.
    deshojadas.

De los árboles desnudos
la vestidura luciente
    primorosa
ya de aquilones sañudos
arrebata la corriente
    presurosa.

Al melancólico suelo
ya la lumbre del sol bella
    no aparece:
lleno de sombras el cielo,
en las noches ni una estrella
    resplandece.

Ya la lluvia se derrama
entre la amarilla grama,
    y acrecienta
la desolada tristura

Song [2]

Faded with autumn
are the bright and clear
    dawns,
the summer flowers
sleep bare in shaded
    vales.

The raging northern
wind's furious blasts
    strip
the brilliant garments
from the uncovered
    trees.

The sunlight forsakes
the melancholy
    soil:
in the dark night sky
not a single star
    shines.

A trickle of rain
on the yellowed grass
    adds
to the emptiness

que en la desierta llanura
    se presenta.

El campo tristeza ofrece
y la ciudad enfadosa
    tedio inspira:
tú mis horas embellece,
compañera deliciosa,
    blanda lira.

Otros busquen en buen hora
la dicha de sus amores
    ponderada;
¡tú con risa encantadora
me darás dichas mayores
    retirada!

Otros oigan extasiados
acentos enamorados,
    ¡lira mía!;
sólo a mí tu canto grave
o tu murmurio suave
    me extasía.

Poesías (1852)

of the deserted
    fields.

The city offers
boredom; the country,
    grief:
you, delightful friend,
enrich my hours, sweet
    lyre.

Let others search for
the tranquil joy of
    love;
With charming smiles, you
will give me greater
    bliss!

Let others be thrilled
with amorous songs;
    lyre,
your solemn and soft
sounds enthrall none
    but me.

El espino

Yo no quiero de los campos
los árboles ni las parras
ni la multitud vistosa
de sus bellísimas plantas;

pero un espino florido
que hay, Emilio, entre las zarzas,
es la envidia de mis ojos
la codicia de mi alma.

Viste su tronco ramaje
de verdes hojas lozanas,
y entre sus brazos airosos
flores como espumas alza.

Más ansiosa que la abeja
en su perfume embriagada,
vago errante, sin aliento,
en torno de sus guirnaldas.

Mas, tiendo en vano los brazos
que antes que llegue alcanzarlas
los punzadoras espinas
de sus ramos me desgarran.

The Hawthorn

I care not for either
the fields' trees or their vines
or for the bright array
of their exquisite plants;

but, Emilio, my eyes
covet and my soul craves
a flowery hawthorn
surrounded by brambles.

Abundant green foliage
beautifies its trunk, and
blooms ascend like sea foam
from its graceful branches.

Like a spirited bee
excited by its scent,
I flitter aimlessly,
breathless, around its wreath.

In vain I lift my arms
because the spiny thorns
of its branches pierce me
before I reach the bloom.

Huye la flor de mis manos;
crece de mi pecho el ansia;
la flor queda en el espino
y en el espino mis lágrimas.

Ermita de Bótoa, 1844

Poesías (1852)

The bloom evades my hands;
my heart beats anxiously;
the bloom clings to the shrub
and my tears do the same.

Ermita de Bótoa, 1844

¡Primavera invisible!

¡Qué caso tan peregrino
un año sin primavera!...
Pasó sin que yo la viera
¿o es tal vez mi desatino?

¿Que bandos de ruiseñores
en la arboleda cantaron
y que a millares brotaron
y se agostaron las flores?

¿De qué modo, cómo, cuándo
eso pasó, Emilio, di?
O yo nada percebí
o todo lo estás soñando.

¿Qué tamaña desventura
me gritaba en los oídos
que de esos claros sonidos
ni el rumor sentí, criatura?

¿Adónde estaban mis ojos
que no han visto en los collados
tantos lirios azulados
y tantos pimpollos rojos?

Invisible Spring!

What a peculiar case,
a year that has no spring!
Did it pass by unseen
or am I mistaken?

Did flocks of nightingales
sing in the thicket and
did millions of flowers
first blossom and then wilt?

How and when, Emilio,
did this happen, tell me?
Either I saw nothing
or it was just your dream.

What terrible mishap
filled my ears with loud shouts,
for me not to notice
these distinct sounds, my child?

Where were my eyes so I
did not see the hillocks
covered with blue lilies
and so many red buds?

¡Yo que soñaba impaciente
con la nueva primavera!
¡Yo que su rosa primera
aguardaba atentamente!

¡Perderla así de ese modo
sin haberla contemplado!...
¡Ay, Emilio!, yo he cegado
o tú lo has soñado todo.

De las bellas estaciones
adoro, Emilio, el placer,
y no quisiera perder
ni un solo de sus dones.

Mas sin duda comprimidos
con fortísima tristeza
yo he tenido en mi cabeza
medio muertos los sentidos.

Y cuando al cabo despierto
de mi letargo penoso
hallo un estío ardoroso
y hallo un campo ya desierto.

Ansia de felicidad,
me devora el alma mía,

I, who impatiently
dreamt about the new spring!
I, who watched carefully
for the rose's first bloom!

Having spring pass by and
not be looking at it! . . .
Am I blinded, or did you,
Emilio, dream it all?

Each lovely season has
a pleasure I adore,
Emilio, and I hate
to miss even one gift.

No doubt my mind was gripped
by a profound sadness,
which left all my feelings
in a state of stupor.

When at last I awoke
from my painful torpor,
I found a hot summer
and a desolate field.

A hope for happiness
devours this soul of mine,

mas por acaso me guía
su instinto a la adversidad.

Y yo pienso que ha de ser
porque en mi pecho doliente
alienta imperfectamente
el sentido del placer.

Y amo, y busco la aflicción
porque en su grande sentir
a sus anchuras latir
puede sólo el corazón.

Por eso los ruiseñores
que sonaron no escuché,
ni he visto, aunque las busqué
en los campos, esas flores.

Por eso la primavera,
que tú dices que pasó,
aunque la aguardaba yo
pasó sin que yo la viera.

Ermita de Bótoa, 1846

Poesías (1852)

yet my instinct guides me
toward adversity.

And I think it must be
that a sense of pleasure
finds little nourishment
in my suffering heart.

I adore and seek out
affliction, for that grand
feeling alone allows
a heart to beat fully.

This is why I did not
hear the nightingales sing,
and why I did not find
those flowers in the fields.

This is why I missed it,
though you say it happened,
and after my long wait,
I did not see spring pass.

Ermita de Bótoa, 1846

Gloria de las flores

Si las flores del jardín
mueren, joven, con el día,
también las de mi poesía
muerte igual tendrán al fin
aunque un poco más tardía.

De abejas la turba ahora
el *ramillete* florido
de mis cantares adora;
mas cuando hayan perecido
abejas, arpa y cantora,

tras los años destructores,
¿sabes tú si de esas flores
que hoy brota mi pensamiento
no se habrá llevado el viento
hojas, aroma y colores?

Más corto o más prolongado
a todos ha señalado
la suerte en la tierra fin;
muere la flor del jardín
después que la flor del prado,

Glory of the Flowers

If the garden flowers
die young with the setting sun,
my poetic flowers
will suffer the same fate
after a brief reprise.

Today the swarm of bees
admires the blooming
bouquet of my songs, but
when bees, harp, and singer
have perished with time

and devastating years,
do you think the flowers
blooming within my mind
will not yield their fragrance,
leaves, and hues to the wind?

Now or anon, mortals
are fated to end their
terrestrial existence;
the garden flowers die
as do the wildflowers.

y aunque un poco más tardía
quiera acercarse la muerte,
a la flor de mi poesía
también de la misma suerte
ha de llegarle su día.

Porque otros hombres vendrán
y mi libro carcomido
por acaso no verán,
o de mi ramo querido
las flores desdeñarán.

Y marchito, deshojado
como las flores del prado
y las flores del jardín,
con ellas quedará al fin
mi ramillete enterrado.

Badajoz, 1845

Poesías (1852)

Even if death chooses
to delay gathering
my poetic flowers,
they, too, in the same way,
will face that fateful day.

For others will come who
perhaps will overlook
my worm-eaten book or
disdain the flowers of
my beloved bouquet.

Wilted and without leaves,
much like the wildflowers
and those of the garden,
my poetic bouquet
will end buried with them.

Badajoz, 1845

Bendito seas, Alberto

Aunque serena y callada
a tus suspiros me veas,
no indiferente me creas;
es que el alma enamorada
diciendo está embelesada
Alberto, bendito seas.

Si a responderte no acierto
cuando me vienes hablando,
¿piensas que tu voz no advierto?
pues es que estoy murmurando
con un acento muy blando
Bendito seas, Alberto.

Alberto, ¿qué más deseas
de quien tanto vive amando?
yo te ruego que me creas,
que aunque callada me veas
estoy entre mí cantando
Alberto, bendito seas.

Muda estoy, fáltame vida;
queda el espíritu muerto,
la mente desvanecida;

Praise to You, Alberto

Though you see me quiet
and serene, it is not
unconcern for your sighs,
rather, my soul in love,
saying rapturously,
Alberto, praise to you.

If I do not answer
when you speak close to me,
have I not heard your voice?
Rather, I am saying
softly within myself,
Praise to you, Alberto.

What more do you expect
from one who loves so much?
I beg you, believe me
though you see me silent,
inside I am singing
Alberto, praise to you.

I fall mute, my life ebbs;
my spirit is dying,
my mind begins to fade;

pero esta voz repetida
forma en el alma concierto:
¡Bendito seas, Alberto!

Elvas, 1845

Poesías (1852)

but this persistent voice

creates my soul's concert:

Praise to you, Alberto!

Elvas, 1845

¡Oh, cuál te adoro!

¡Oh, cuál te adoro! con la luz del día
tu nombre invoco apasionada y triste,
y cuando el cielo en sombra se reviste
aún te llama exaltada el alma mía.

¡Tú eres el tiempo que mis horas guía,
tú eres la idea que a mi mente asiste,
porque en ti se encuentra cuanto existe,
mi pasión, mi esperanza, mi poesía!

No hay canto que igualar pueda tu acento
cuando tu amor me cuentas y deliras,
revelando la fe de tu contento;

tiemblo a tu voz y tiemblo si me miras,
y quisiera exhalar mi último aliento
abrasada en el aire que respiras.

Badajoz, 1845
Poesías (1852)

Oh, How I Adore You!

Oh, how I adore you! At dawn's birth
I invoke you with passion and grief,
and when the sky drapes itself in black,
my elated soul still calls to you.

You are the time that directs my hours,
the idea that nourishes my mind,
in you all existence is contained,
my fervor, my hope, my poetry.

No chant can equal your song when you
declare your love for me with rapture
making your contentment manifest;

I tremble at your voice and your gaze,
and I hope to draw my dying breath
consumed by flames in the air you breathe.

Badajoz, 1845

Siempre tú

La niebla del diciembre quebrantaba
del sol los melancólicos fulgores
cuando en mi corazón de tus amores
el acento primero resonaba.

El segundo diciembre se acercaba
trayendo para mí nieblas mayores
que a merced de los vientos bramadores
tu nave en el Atlántico bogaba.

Y el diciembre tercero aparecía
templado, alegre como el mayo hermoso
y eras tú mi suspiro todavía.

El cuarto arrebatado, tempestuoso,
vino a robarme la ventura mía
¡ay! mas no a dar a mi pasión reposo.

Badajoz, 1846

Poesías (1852)

Forever You

The fog of December broke
the sun's melancholy glow
when first my heart resounded
with the echoes of your love.

When December reappeared,
heavy fog rolled in for me
as your ship braved the rage of
the Atlantic's roaring winds.

And the third December came,
mild and cheerful like lovely
May, and still for you I pined.

The fourth, rash and turbulent,
alas, came to seize my joy,
but brought my passion no rest.

Badajoz, 1846

¡No hay nada más triste que el último adiós!

Si dos con el alma se amaron en vida
y al fin se separan en vida los dos,
sabéis que es tan grande la pena sentida
que nada hay más triste que el último ¡adiós!

En esa palabra que breve murmuran,
en ese gemido que exhalan los dos,
ni verse prometen, ni amarse se juran,
que en esa palabra se dicen ¡adiós!

No hay queja más honda, suspiro más largo
que aquella palabra que dicen los dos:
el alma se entrega a horrible letargo;
la vida se acaba diciéndose ¡adiós!

Al fin ha llegado la muerte en la vida,
y al fin para entrambos morimos los dos;
al fin ha llegado la hora cumplida
la hora más triste... el último ¡adiós!

Saddest of All Is the Last Farewell!

If two souls in life loved each other
and yet in their lifetime they must part—
you sense the depth of the pain because
saddest of all is the last "farewell"!

With that brief word they whisper softly,
with that moan they both exhale and vow
not to meet, not to love each other,
with that word they are saying "farewell"!

No complaint rings more profound, no sigh
deeper than that word they both declaim;
the soul gives itself to weariness;
life comes to an end saying "farewell"!

And now the living death has arrived
and now we both die for each other,
and now the decisive hour has struck,
oh, the saddest hour . . . the last "farewell"!

Ya nunca en la vida, gentil compañero,
ya nunca volveremos a vernos los dos;
por eso es tan triste mi acento postrero,
que nada hay más triste que el último ¡adiós!

Cádiz, 1847

Poesías (1852)

No more in life, gentle companion,
are the two of us to meet again;
that is why my tone tolls sadly now,
saddest of all is the last "farewell"!

Cádiz, 1847

Nada resta de ti

Nada resta de ti... te hundió el abismo...
te tragaron los monstruos de los mares.
No quedan en los fúnebres lugares
ni los huesos siquiera de ti mismo.

Fácil de comprender, amante Alberto,
es que perdieras en el mar la vida,
mas no comprende el alma dolorida
cómo yo vivo cuando tú ya has muerto.

¡¡Darnos la vida a mí y a ti la muerte;
darnos a ti la paz y a mí la guerra;
dejarte a ti en el mar y a mí en la tierra,
es la maldad más grande de la suerte!!...

Cádiz, 1848

Poesías (1852)

No Trace of You

No trace of you . . . sunk in the abyss . . .
swallowed up by monsters of the sea;
no trace of you, not even your bones
to be put to rest in hallowed ground.

It is clear, beloved Alberto,
you have given your life to the sea,
but my grieving soul will ne'er conceive
how I am alive when you are dead.

To have given me life and you death;
to give you concord and me discord;
to leave you at sea and me on shore,
is destiny's greatest villainy!

Cádiz, 1848

Amistad de la luna

Esa oscura enfermedad
que llaman melancolía
me trajo a la soledad
a verte, luna sombría.

Ya seas amante doncella
ya informe, negro montón
de tierra que en forma bella
nos convierte la ilusión.

Ni a sorprender tus amores
mis tristes ojos vinieron
ni a saber si esos fulgores
son tuyos o te los dieron.

Ni a mí me importa que esté
tu luz viva o desmayada,
ni cuando te miro sé
si eres roja o plateada.

Yo busco tu compañía
porque al fin, muda beldad,
es tu amistad menos fría
que otra cualquiera amistad.

The Moon's Friendship

This somber malady,
known as melancholy,
carried me here to you,
dark moon, in solitude.

Are you a romantic
maiden or shapeless mass
of black earth, made lovely
for us by illusion?

My sad eyes do not seek
to catch you with your loves
or to know if your glow
reflects or radiates.

Whether you shine or pale
or whether your color
sparkles red or silver
matters little to me.

I long to be near you
because, silent beauty,
your friendship chills me less
than other affections,

Sé bien que todo el poder
de tu misterioso encanto
no alcanzará a detener
una gota de mi llanto.

Mas yo no guardo consuelos
para este mal tan profundo.
Fijo la vista en los cielos
porque me importuna el mundo...

¡Vergüenza del mundo es
si tiene mi pensamiento
que ir a buscarte al través
de las nubes y del viento,

y llevar hasta tu esfera
mi solitaria armonía
para hallar la compañera
que escucha la pena mía!

Mas, pues no me da la fortuna
otra más tierna amistad,
vengo con mis penas, luna,
a verte en la soledad.

Ermita de Bótoa, 1846

Poesías (1852)

even if the force of
your elusive allure
cannot arrest the flow
of a single teardrop.

As I find no solace
for my profound sorrow,
my eyes turn heavenward
for my distress on earth . . .

Oh, shame upon the world
if my thoughts must embark
and go in search of you
behind both clouds and wind,

and carry my lone plea
to your exalted sphere
to find a soulmate who
will listen to my woes!

But, since fortune gave me
no other loving friend,
I bring you my laments,
O moon, in solitude.

Ermita de Bótoa, 1846

Robustiana Armiño
(1821–90)
Robustiana Armiño Menéndez de Cuesta

The daughter of a pharmacist, Robustiana Armiño was born in Gijón, a port city in the northern Spanish province of Asturias. She corresponded with several other women poets, above all with Carolina Coronado. In her *Poesías* (1851), Armiño dedicated poems to Coronado and Gertrudis Gómez de Avellaneda, another poet she greatly admired. Coronado, who wrote the introduction to Armiño's collected poems, praised the Asturian poet's efforts to overcome her lack of a formal education, including teaching herself foreign languages. After her marriage to Juan de la Cuesta Cherner, Armiño abandoned poetry but continued publishing other writings, usually with a moral message. From 1869 to 1872 she contributed articles to a conservative weekly, *Altar y trono* ("Altar and Throne") and became the editor of *La familia* in 1875.

Her poem "Plegaria" ("Supplication"), which shows her strong religious inclination, is also a representative sample of the intimate relationship many nineteenth-century women poets felt with the Virgin Mary.

Plegaria

Hay en mi corazón un pensamiento,
pensamiento de amor, de luz y vida,
¡reina del elevado firmamento!
trueca mi amor en fuego celestial.
Si arrancas de mi pecho la belleza
que trastornó mi débil fantasía,
¿quién en el mundo entonces, ¡oh María!
amará más tu rostro virginal?

Escucha mi clamor, flor de las flores.
Paz es el bien que anhela el alma mía;
cual estrella oriental serás mi guía,
serás la inspiración de mis amores;
serás fuente de bien y de consuelos;
yo elevaré a tu gloria mis cantares,
y tú darás alivio a mis pesares,
enviándome tu luz desde los cielos.

Tus cándidos querubes
pulsarán con placer la lira mía,
y los ardientes versos
con que se exhala en cánticos diversos
un triste corazón
te serán ¡oh María! dirigidos,
y en el sereno día

Supplication

In my heart there lives a thought,
a thought of life, light, and love,
O heavenly queen, transform
my love to celestial fire!
If from my heart you banish
the beauty that beguiled me,
then who else could, O Mary,
love your virginal face more?

Hear my plea, divine flower.
Peace is what my soul desires;
guide me like the eastern star,
inspire my loves, be the source
of my goodness and solace;
my songs will praise your glory
and you will ease my sorrows,
sending me your sacred light.

Your candid cherubs
will strum my harp with pleasure,
and the passionate
verses with which a sad heart
composes its hymns
will be for you, O Mary;
during the calm day

y en la plácida noche,
cuando ilumina la creciente luna
la misteriosa flor de la laguna,
tú serás mi sublime inspiración.

Poesías, vol. 2

and the peaceful night
when the waxing moon shines on
the lagoon's exotic bloom,
you will be my sublime muse.

La tempestad

¿Qué legión infernal los aires hiende
lanzando por doquier hondo gemido,
porque al rayo de un sol descolorido
maléfico vapor al mar desciende?

La atrevida gaviota el vuelo tiende,
tiembla el globo en sus ejes conmovido,
de las hinchadas olas el bramido
súbita catarata se desprende.

Brilla en el éter misteriosa lumbre,
estalla el huracán… , retumba el trueno
sobre las alas de aquilón sañudo…

Póstrase ante el altar la muchedumbre,
de angustioso pavor el pecho lleno.
Sublime tempestad, yo te saludo.

Safo en Castilla (ed. Vázquez de Aldana)

The Tempest

Which infernal legion rifts the air,
hurling its intense groans everywhere,
as a maleficent mist descends
to the sea by the fading sunlight?

The daring seagull rises in flight,
the sphere trembles, its axis shaken;
in the roar, the swollen waves release
a swiftly cascading waterfall.

A mystical glow brightens the sky,
the hurricane explodes . . . thunder rolls
on the wings of an enraged north wind.

The throng kneels down before the altar,
an anguished terror grips every heart—
majestic tempest, I salute you!

Ángela Grassi
(1823–83)
Ángela Grassi y Techi de Cuenca

When she was six, Ángela Grassi moved to Spain with her father, the Italian musician Juan Grassi y de Lucia. She began her literary career with a successful drama in 1842, and during the next decade she wrote both plays and poetry. After 1860, she authored numerous sentimental and moralistic novels, which first appeared in serial form in *El correo de la moda*, a weekly magazine owned by her husband, Victor Cuenca, and edited by her. In her widely read novels and stories, she stressed domesticity and fostered a conservative view of women's role in society. Her poem "Despedida" ("The Farewell") was written around 1851, a year after the publication of Gertrudis Gómez de Avellaneda's poem "A ***," and there are striking similarities between the two works.

La despedida

¡Hubo un tiempo te amé! ¡Dentro del pecho
un altar te eregí: tú eras el solo
único objeto de mi ardiente culto,
mi sumo bien, mi religión, mi todo!
En ti cifraba mi existencia entera,
por ti el vivir me pareció dichoso,
bella la muerte, que al amor le es dado
con su llama avivar el yerto polvo.
¿Qué me importaba de esa ciega turba
el aplauso o desdén? Para ti solo
inmarcesible lauro ambicionaba
y un renombre inmortal del mundo asombro.
¡Cuánto te amé! Pendiente de tu labio,
me viste estremecer, temblar de gozo,
cuando tu voz tan desdeñosa siempre
formulaba de amor sagrado voto.
¡En vano mi mirada escrutadora
doquier buscaba con empeño loco
otro mortal más digno de mi afecto,
digno cual tú del general encomio!
¡Engañosa ilusión! ¡El bello manto
que al ídolo fatal sirvió de adorno
el tiempo disipó!... ¡Vi convertido
en tímido mortal al gran coloso!
¡Del pedestal caíste en que mi mano

The Farewell

There was a time I loved you! I built
an altar for you in my heart, and
you were the sole object of my cult,
my supreme bliss, religion, my all!
My whole existence revolved around
you; because of you, life seemed joyous
and death beautiful, since with its flame
love can revive even lifeless dust.
What did it matter to me if I
received the blind mob's praise or disdain?
For you alone I sought undying
laurels and eternal worldly fame.
How I adored you! Trembling, I hung
on your words, and joy overcame me
when your voice, always so disdainful,
expressed a promise of sacred love.
In vain I hunted everywhere with
anxious eagerness for another
mortal worthy of my affection,
one who'd be as praiseworthy as you.
Oh deceitful illusion! With time,
the lovely cloak adorning the false
idol faded! . . . I saw the giant
transformed into a timorous man.
You have fallen from the pedestal

te colocó insensata, y cual oprobio
recuerdo el llanto que por ti he vertido
al mirar tu desdén y tu abandono!
¿Conoces tú el amor? Sabes acaso
lo que encierra este nombre tan hermoso,
que es fuente eterna de entusiasmo inmenso,
de abnegación purísimo tesoro?
¡Ay, no lo sabes, no!… Tu pecho frío
no comprende ese afecto, y por el lodo
de vil materialismo calcinado,
cálculo y falsedad sólo ve en torno!
¡Tu talento sin par puede altanero
los átomos contar del ancho globo,
pero tu corazón seco y marchito
en misterios de amor jamás fue docto!
¡Indigno eres de mí!… ¿De nieve helada
cuando ardiente volcán pudo ser socio?
¡Lo que te sobra en calculada ciencia,
en corazón me sobra generoso!
¡Vano el empeño es ya! El amante lazo
que nos unió fatal tranquila rompo:
¡Hoy no me ves llorar!… ¡Hoy que el desprecio
con que acoges mi amor pusiste el colmo!
¡Mírame sonreír… mírame alegre
entre el bullicio rebosar de gozo,
y ni un instante tu *adorada imagen*
se presentó fatal ante mis ojos!

on which my hand naively placed you;
seeing your scorn and abandonment,
I recall with shame the tears I shed.
Do you know what love is? Do you know
the meaning of this enchanting word,
eternal fount of immense fervor,
purest treasure of abnegation?
Oh no, you do not know! . . . Your cold heart
cannot grasp this feeling, for hardened
by vile materialism, it sees
only falsehood and calculation.
With unsurpassed talent you proudly
count all the atoms in the wide world
but never has your dry and withered
heart been well versed in love's mysteries.
You're unworthy of me! How can ice
be next to a burning volcano?
You know more about the sciences,
but my heart is far more generous.
All efforts are now in vain! Calmly
I break the ties that joined us in love.
Today you won't see me cry . . . today
you've shown my love your fullest contempt!
Look at me smile . . . see how I rejoice
amid a boisterous commotion,
without having your *adored image*
even an instant before my eyes.

¡Pasó aquel tiempo ya!... ¡Pasó aquel tiempo
en que tu esclava fui!... ¡Hoy sin encono
puedo decirte que en tu ausencia vivo
y hallo placeres, si el placer evoco!
¡De hoy más tu nombre que adoré ferviente
no vibrará en mi pecho melodioso;
será un nombre no más, un nombre vano
que no revela ni cariño ni odio!
¡Ya para siempre adiós! ¡y ojalá nunca
recuerdes al luchar contra el insomnio,
que nadie como yo supo adorarte,
y me pagaste con mezquino dolo!
¡No lo recuerdes, no! El remordimiento
es cáncer que devora ponzoñoso;
recuerda sólo que al dejar de amarte
exclamé sin rencor: *¡yo te perdono!*

Poesías

That time has passed! Gone is the time when
I was your slave. Today I can say
without rancor that in your absence
I live and find the pleasures I choose!
Hence your name—once fervently adored—
will no longer echo in my heart;
it will merely be an empty name,
revealing neither fondness nor hate.
Farewell forever! I hope you don't
spend your sleepless hours remembering
that no one loved you as much as I
and that you paid me with vile deceit.
No, don't remember it! Remorse is
a venomous cancer that devours;
remember only that when I ceased
loving you, I said, *"I forgive you."*

Amalia Fenollosa

(1825–69)

Amalia Fenollosa y Peris

A precocious poet, Amalia Fenollosa began writing poetry at age eleven, and when she was thirteen, she composed an elegy on the death of her father. Her collected verse, *Poesías* (1843), appearing the same year as Carolina Coronado's first volume of poetry, is among the earliest publications of feminine poetry in the nineteenth century. Yet the many poems that Fenollosa contributed to various literary magazines after 1843 were not available in book form until their publication in 2002. After her marriage in 1851 to the newspaper editor and university professor Joan Manyé i Flaquer, she gave up her literary endeavors and dedicated herself to her family. She died at forty-four after a long battle with cancer.

"Soneto," in which Fenollosa expresses her affection for her friend and fellow poet Manuela Cambronero, is a typical example of the poems exchanged by members of the Lyrical Sisterhood. In "Mis celos" ("A Lover's Jealousy"), the masculine speaking voice uses the description of the many manifestations of his jealousy as a pretext for paying tribute to his beloved and to nature.

Soneto

A la señorita Manuela Cambronero, remitiéndole una flor

Esa flor que lozana y agraciada
en mi lindo jardín brilló algún día,
esa flor que brillante humedecía
con gotas de rocío la alborada,

esa flor que en mi seno aprisionada
deliciosos perfumes despedía,
y que hora le envío hermana mía
cual dulce prenda de amistad sagrada,

esa flor es emblema de tu vida
grata algún tiempo, deliciosa y pura
antes de ser por el amor herida,

hoy marchita y cubierta de amargura,
logrando como dicha apetecida
tus besos, como logras mi ternura.

Castellón, el 25 de marzo de 1845

Poesías

Sonnet

To Miss Manuela Cambronero, upon sending her a flower

This luxurious flower that bloomed
one day in my beautiful garden,
this flower that the early morning
moistened with iridescent dewdrops,

this flower that, fastened to my breast,
released aromatic fragrances,
I send to you now, sister of mine,
as a sweet sign of sacred friendship.

This flower is emblematic of
your life, once so spotless, delightful,
and pleasant before love wounded it;

now wilted and filled with bitterness,
it hopes to win the bliss of your kiss
just as you have won my tenderness.

Castellón, 25 March 1845

A un ángel

Bello querubo cuya casta frente
nevosa brilla entre tus rizos de oro,
dulce cantar que en el celeste coro
tu voz elevas sin igual y ardiente.

Si mi súplica tierna y vehemente,
si mi continuo y angustiado lloro,
este lugar enlutan donde moro
de pena hinchado mi pensar ferviente

sé tu mi protector, con tu sonrisa
aleja el soplo del pensar insano
que ya en delirio por momentos frisa.

Tiéndeme en mi orfandad tu suave mano
y con tu aliento de ligera brisa
calma piadoso mi dolor tirano.

Poesías

To an Angel

Beautiful cherub, whose chaste brow casts
snowy beams beneath your golden curls,
you raise your unique and ardent voice
in the celestial choir's pleasing song.

If my passionate and tender plea,
my anguished and persistent laments
envelop in mourning the abode
where I live with sorrow-laden thoughts,

be my protector and with your smile
save my mind from the gusts of madness
that threaten it in fevered moments.

Offer your kind hand to this orphan
and with your breath like an airy breeze
mercifully soothe my ruthless pain.

Un adiós

Bramó la tempestad; fiero, iracundo
 tendió Aquilón sus alas.
Estremecióse a su fragor el mundo,
 perdió el campo sus galas.
Sorprendida en los brazos de su amado
 la tímida paloma.
Huyó temblando su poder airado
 que los cedros desploma.
Y rendida después, cansado el vuelo,
 de su par separada,
cayó por fin en el estéril suelo
 de selva enmarañada.
Tal enmedio del mágico delirio
 de una pasión ardiente,
sopló para los dos el seco sirio
 de mi suerte inclemente.
Enemigos del amor nos separaron
 matando mi albedrío.
¿Por qué entonces no traspasaron
 tu corazón y el mío?
Con su falsa piedad vivir me mandan,
 vivir sin tus amores
¡Ah, mis fervientes lágrimas no ablandan
 su encono y sus furores!

A Farewell

The storm raged; the fierce North Wind spread
his angry wings.
The world shook with the sound; the fields
lost their grandeur.
The timid dove was caught in her
lover's embrace.
Trembling she fled from the fury
that felled cedars.
Fatigued from flight, separated
from her beloved,
she plummeted to the bare ground
of tangled brush.
Thus, amid the enchantment of
fevered passion,
the dry wind of my ill fortune
tore us apart.
Foes of love separated us,
against my will.
Then why didn't they also pierce
your heart and mine?
Falsely pious, they told me: Live!
Without your love?
My fervent tears can't soften their
fury and ire.

¡Adiós Rugiero! La paloma herida
    es hoy la que te amaba.
Si la querías tú, ¡su despedida
    sobre tu pecho graba!

Castellón de la Plana, el 27 de abril de 1849

Poesías

Farewell, Rugiero! This wounded
dove once loved you.
If you loved her too, her good-bye
etch in your heart!

Castellón de la Plana, 27 April 1849

Mis celos

Cuando anoche en el jardín
tibia luna reflejaba
y extasiado contemplaba
tu semblante seductor,
    cuando la brisa en sus alas
movía tus blondos rizos
y el imán de tus hechizos
me embriagaba de amor,
    cuando oía de tus labios
dulces frases de ternura
acentos de un alma pura
que el dolo no conoció,
    yo dichoso me creía
con tan mágico embeleso,
y allí entre el follaje espeso
mi mente se enloqueció.
    Mas pronto una idea vaga
vino a turbar mis sentidos
entonces embebecidos
de tus gracias al poder.
    Y esta idea, vagos celos
me sugirió maldecida,
mientras mi dicha querida
huyó para no volver.
    Celos tuve del arroyo

A Lover's Jealousy

When in the garden last night
the mellow moon reflected
your seductive countenance
and with joy I gazed at it,
    when the breeze disheveled your
blond curls with her wings, and I,
attracted by your lures, was
intoxicated with love,
    when from your lips I heard sweet
expressions of tenderness,
tones from an innocent soul
that had never known deceit,
    I thought I was transported
with magical enchantment,
and amid the dense foliage
I felt the rush of madness.
    But soon a vague idea came
to disturb my senses, drunk
in that instant with your charms
that had overpowered them.
    And this cursed idea inspired
nameless jealousies in me,
while my cherished delight fled,
never to return again.
    I was jealous of the stream

que tu imagen retratando
la iba lascivo besando
con audacia sin igual.
Celos del céfiro leve
que en ti jugaba liviano,
celos ¡ay! aunque era en vano,
de algún fantasma ideal.
Celos tuve de los astros
que bordan la azul esfera
porque te ven donde quiera
cuando no me es dado a mí.
Celos del árbol, que apoyo
prestaba a tu noble frente,
celos del prado riente,
celos del blando alhelí.
En todo encontré rivales
que te aman cual te adoro,
a ti, mi solo tesoro,
deidad de mi juventud.
Y lloroso, amante y ciego,
con el alma hecha pedazos,
me separé de tus brazos
en silenciosa actitud.

16 de junio de 1850

Poesías

that, reflecting your image,
kissed it lasciviously with
shameless and wanton boldness.

I was jealous of the soft
zephyr that lightly teased you,
jealous, even though in vain,
oh, of some ideal phantom.

I was jealous of the stars
bordering the azure sphere,
for, wherever you go, they
see you, although I cannot.

I was jealous of the tree
on which you leaned your forehead,
jealous of the cheerful fields
and the gentle wallflower.

To me they all seemed rivals
who love you as much as I
adore you, my sole treasure
and the goddess of my youth.

And, blinded by love and tears,
my heart shattered in pieces,
in silence, I thus withdrew
myself from your embraces.

16 June 1850

Rogelia León
(1828–70)

This Andalusian poet was the dedicatee of several poems by another member of the Lyrical Sisterhood, Vicente García Miranda, with whom she carried on an extensive correspondence. Rogelia León dedicated her collected poems, *Auras de la Alhambra* (1857; "Gentle Breezes from the Alhambra"), to her friend Eduarda Moreno Morales, who like her was a native of Granada. León, who taught at Granada's lyceum, belonged to Círculo Científico, Literario y Artístico de Málaga ("Málaga's Scientific, Literary, and Artistic Circle") and was an honorary member of Academia Científico-Literaria de Madrid ("Madrid's Scientific and Literary Academy"). In her poem "Una española a su amante" ("From a Young Spanish Woman to Her Beloved"), the feminine voice speaks with surprising fervor about the glories of combat, not only encouraging her beloved to take up arms but also vowing to accompany him and even lay down her life if he is killed.

Una española a su amante

Parte a la guerra, sí, parte a la guerra,
con ínclito denuedo allí pelea,
el ámbito conquista de la tierra
y arrójalo a mis pies como presea.

Del cañón el mugido no me aterra,
pues siento que en mi pecho arde la tea
que el glorioso entusiasmo ardiente encierra
y al querer estallar, rojiza humea.

Parte, yo te acompaño, fiel guerrero,
no te detenga aquí mi sentimiento,
que escuche yo crujir el fuerte acero

recostada en el ancho campamento,
y si mueres cual noble caballero,
contigo entregaré mi último aliento.

Auras

From a Young Spanish Woman to Her Beloved

March off to the war, yes, march off
to fight with heroic valor,
conquer the terrestrial sphere and
fling it at my feet like a gem.

I do not fear the cannon's roar,
for passionate fervor has lit
a torch in my heart that exudes
red-hot smoke, wanting to explode.

March off, and I will march with you,
staunch soldier; my feelings should not
stop you. There on the battlefield,

let me hear the clash of steel, and
if you die like a noble knight,
I will draw my last breath with yours.

Manuela Cambronero

Manuela María Cambronero de la Peña

Little is known about this poet, born either in Valladolid or the Galician city of La Coruña, and her year of birth is a speculation based on the dates of her published works. Manuela María Cambronero dedicated a short novel to her close friend and fellow poet Amalia Fenollosa. Her only collected work, *Días de convalescencia* (1852; "Days of Convalescence"), which included both her novels and poems, is dedicated to her husband. The title alludes to the ill health from which the couple suffered at the time of the book's publication.

The closing lines of Cambronero's "La cautiva" ("The Captive"), in which the beautiful speaker bemoans her loss of freedom, echo these verses from José de Espronceda's poem by the same title: "entre doradas cadenas / que si bien de encanto llenas, / al cabo cadenas son" (*Obras poéticas*, ed. Leonardo Romero Tobar [Barcelona: RBA, 1994] 64; "amid golden chains, / which, though filled with delights, / are chains nonetheless").

La cautiva

Tengo perlas y diamantes
relumbrantes,
ciñe corona mi sien;
tengo sedas y bordados
delicados,
ámbar y coral también.

Cien esclavas me acompañan
y me bañan
en esencia de clavel,
llamándome fresca rosa,
primorosa,
luz y encanto del vergel.

La palmera me da sombra;
y en la alfombra
del espléndido jardín,
me reclino entre las flores
de colores
y el blanquísimo jazmín.

Aunque no soy africana,
soy sultana,
y me adora mi señor,
en tanto que otras se afanan

The Captive

I have diamonds and pearls
that sparkle,
and a crown on my head;
finest embroideries,
dainty silks,
amber and coral, too.

One hundred slaves surround
and bathe me
in floral-scented oils,
calling me a graceful
and fresh rose,
the garden's light and charm.

The palm tree shades me as
I recline
on the magnificent
garden rug amid the
colorful
flowers and white jasmine.

A sultana, though not
African,
adored by my master,
while others, dressed in fine

y engalanan,
sin poder lograr su amor.

Envidian una ventura
que maldigo sin cesar.
¡Ah! malhaya mi hermosura,
que es causa de mi pesar.

Está marchita mi frente,
yo no hallo felicidad,
y recuerdo tristemente
mi perdida libertad.

Miro el agua transparente
del arroyo bullicioso
deslizarse suavemente
por el prado delicioso,

y en la rama temblorosa
a el amante ruiseñor,
y la bella mariposa
volando de flor en flor.

Pero la verde pradera
y el aromoso jardín,
la risueña primavera
con sus hechizos sin fin,

attire, strive
in vain to gain his love.

They envy good fortune
that I curse ceaselessly.
Oh, damned be my beauty
that causes me this grief.

My forehead is furrowed,
happiness eludes me;
sadly I remember
the freedom I have lost.

I see the clear water
of the boisterous stream
sliding smoothly along
the delightful prairie;

and on the swaying bough,
the tender nightingale;
the lovely butterfly
darting from bloom to bloom.

But the verdant meadows
and the fragrant garden,
even pleasant spring with
its endless magic spells,

nada calmará las penas
de mi triste corazón;
son doradas mis cadenas,
pero al fin… cadenas son.

Días

cannot soothe the sadness
of my sorrowful heart.
Though my chains are golden,
they are chains nonetheless.

Eduarda Moreno Morales

Eduarda Moreno Morales de López-Nuño

Eduarda Moreno Morales taught at the Academy of Fine Arts in her native city of Granada, but the limited biographical information about her does not even include the dates of her birth and death. Her book of poems *Ayes del alma* (1857; "Laments from the Soul") appeared the same year as the collected verses by her good friend Rogelia León. In 1885, Moreno Morales published both a collection of religious poetry and her last known work, a poem dedicated to Granada's patroness, the Virgin of Angustias. The fragment from her poem "Safo" included here is another variation on the theme of Sappho's desperate pining for Phaon. For Moreno Morales, as for some other nineteenth-century women poets, this legendary love story served as a convenient pretext for composing an erotic poem with a feminine speaking voice.

Safo

(fragmento)

Ya sumergióse la luna;
ya las pléyades cayeron.
—Safo

. . . .

Brisas ligeras que corréis los valles,
olas tranquilas del rizado mar,
auras de la mañana, frescas flores
mecidas por el soplo matinal,

¡a mi amado Faón del alma mía
un suspiro de amor dulce llevad!
Decídle que mi espíritu intranquilo
volando en torno a su amor está.

¡Ay! ya la luna sumergióse triste
velando en nubes su tranquila faz,
y las blancas y pálidas estrellas
ya sus reflejos ocultando van.

¿Quién sabe si mañana vuestros rayos
la losa de mi tumba bañaran?
¿Quién sabe si mañana… ? ¡Mas, ay, triste!
quién vuestro arcano descubrir podrá?

Sappho

(excerpt)

> *The moon has made her descent;*
> *the Pleiades have fallen.*
>
> *—Sappho*

. . . .

Soft winds wafting through the vale,
calm waves of the crested sea,
dawning lights and fresh flowers
swaying in the morning air,

to Phaon, love of my heart,
carry an amorous sigh!
Tell him that my restless soul
flutters all around his love.

The sad moon has descended,
veiling her calm face with clouds,
and the stars, so pale and white,
are hiding their reflections.

Who knows, maybe tomorrow
your rays will shine on my grave?
Who knows if . . . ? Oh, the sadness!
Who can know your mystery?

¿Y quién del porvenir triste y sombrío
puede el velo terrible levantar?
Sólo una tumba silenciosa y fría
nuestros tristes delirios calmará.

¡Ven, ven, Faón! ¡La luna sumergióse!
Mi corazón te llama con afán!
¡Un suspiro, un suspiro de tus labios!
Una dulce palabra, nada más.

Yo en cambio te daré mi vida toda,
y un mundo de placer y de verdad,
y el infinito fuego de mi alma,
ardiente como el seno del volcán.

Ayes

Who can lift the dreadful mask
from such a dreary future?
Only a cold and silent
tomb will calm our delirium.

Come, the moon has descended!
Come, Phaon, my heart calls you!
A sigh, a sigh from your lips!
A gentle word, nothing more.

I will give you my whole life,
a world of truth and pleasure,
and my soul's eternal fire,
raging like a volcano.

Faustina Sáez de Melgar
(1834–95)
Faustina Sáez Toro de Melgar

Faustina Sáez de Melgar titled her collected poems *La lira del Tajo* (1859; "The Lyre of the Tajo") in honor of the river that flows by her native town of Villamanrique de Tajo, in the province of Madrid. After her marriage to Valentín Melgar, the couple moved to the capital, where she became a member of the Sociedad Abolicionista Española ("Spanish Abolitionist Society") and presided over the Ateneo Artístico y Literario de Señoras ("Atheneum of Artistic and Literary Ladies"). She contributed her writings, including some novels in serialized form, to numerous literary magazines. Like Carolina Coronado, Sáez de Melgar encouraged contemporary women poets, publishing their works in *La violeta* (1862–66), the journal she founded and edited. In the quartet of poems featured here, each sonnet personifies one of the four seasons in a vivid and charming, if somewhat conventional, manner. Feminine figures alternate with masculine ones as the year progresses from youth (spring) to adulthood (summer), maturity (autumn), and old age (winter).

La primavera

Es una niña cándida y hermosa
de lánguido mirar, dulce semblante,
que con grave apostura y talante,
se presenta risueña y vaporosa.

Con túnica sencilla y misteriosa,
que ondula por doquier leve y radiante,
y dorado cabello, que brillante
flota a merced del aura licensiosa.

Al mostrarse en abril fresca y ligera,
la saludan los pájaros cantores,
y la brisa la arrulla lisonjera,
céfiro requiriéndola de amores.

Su nombre la pregunta: PRIMAVERA,
la niña dice, derramando flores.

La lira

Spring

She's a lovely and candid girl,
with her languid look, gentle face;
though grand in mien and manner, she
is cheerful and ethereal.

Her simple and magic tunic
flutters radiantly in the air;
her golden hair glows, flowing at
the mercy of the teasing breeze.

So fresh and agile in April,
she is welcomed by the songbirds;
the breeze coos a flattering song;
the zephyr clamors for her love.

Asked to give her name, the young girl,
scattering flowers, replies, SPRING.

El estío

¿Adónde vas, viajero peregrino,
por esos abrasados arenales,
ya internándote en densos matorrales,
o incansable siguiendo tu camino?

¿Fijas la vista en el cenit divino,
absorbiendo los rayos estivales,
y en ellos las flores virginales
agostando, cual fiero torbellino?

Vueltos al sol, impávidos los ojos,
con orgullo satánico y bravío,
audaz bebiendo de sus rayos rojos
el volcánico ardor con desvarío.

¿Quién eres, di? porque me das enojos.
Fuego, responde, soy; mi nombre, ESTÍO.

La lira

Summer

Wandering pilgrim, where are you
going along the burning sands,
now entering dense forests, now
following your route without rest?

Is your gaze fixed on the divine
horizon so you can absorb
the sun's rays and parch the virgin
flowers like an enraged whirlwind?

Turned to the sun, eyes unflinching,
with satanic and haughty pride,
you drink the volcanic blaze of
red rays in bold delirium.

Who are you? You disconcert me!
I am fire, my name is SUMMER.

El otoño

¿No véis bajar de pámpanos ceñida
la altiva frente a la matrona bella?
¿No véis que brilla cual radiante estrella
del firmamento en la mansión lucida?

Con dulces frutos de la vid convida
y osados siguen su ondulante huella
mancebos mil apasionados de ella,
con planta asaz ligera y atrevida.

Huid les dice: vuestro empeño en vano,
pretenderme fijar es desatino;
Mi vida es breve, alcánzame el anciano
que marcha en las edades peregrino.

Y yo que del OTOÑO soy emblema,
depongo ante él mi cetro y diadema.

La lira

Autumn

See the lovely matron nearing,
vine leaves crowning her haughty brow?
Don't you see her shine like a star
in heaven's brightly lit mansion?

She offers the grapevine's sweet fruits,
and a thousand impassioned youths
dare to follow her winding trail,
with plucky and light-footed steps.

Flee, she tells them, all is in vain;
it is folly to detain me.
My life is brief; soon the ancient
wanderer will overtake me.

And to him I will relinquish
my scepter and crown of AUTUMN.

El invierno

¿Quién eres, di, anciano macilento
que da pavor tu pálida figura?
Al verte se entristece la natura,
y se escucha doquier hondo lamento.

Se encapota el azul del firmamento,
trocando su color por niebla oscura,
que la llama del sol cubre insegura,
debilitando su ardoroso aliento.

Nace la aurora entre la escarcha fría,
y no hay aves, ni hay flores, no hay aromas;
se respira una atmósfera sombría
que surca solo la torcaz paloma.

¡Huye INVIERNO! y devuelve al claro cielo
su hermoso azul y su esmaltado velo.

La lira

Winter

Who are you, old and wizened man,
whose pale figure inspires fear?
Nature saddens at your sight and
deep laments echo everywhere.

The blue sky dons a black mantle
and the sun's flickering flame is
enveloped in a dark fog that
diminishes its scorching breath.

The morning dawns amid cold frost
with no birds, no flowers, no scents;
alone the ring dove cuts a path
across the gloomy atmosphere.

Return to the sky its lovely
shiny blue veil. Begone, WINTER!

María del Pilar Sinués
(1835–93)
María del Pilar Sinués y Navarro de Marco
Pseudonym: Laura

María del Pilar Sinués was a poet, a journalist, and one of Spain's most prolific and popular writers of domestic novels. She was closely associated with the traditional stereotype of the domestic woman embodied by the *ángel del hogar* ("angel of the hearth"), the title of her most famous work as well as the name of one of the journals she founded. Like other editors of women's magazines (Faustina Sáez de Melgar, Robustiana Armiño, and Ángela Grassi), she intended to educate her female readership. It is sadly ironic that though she advised women on marital issues, her own marriage was unsuccessful and ended in separation. Her mournful ballad "Amor materno" ("A Mother's Love") depicts the plight of a fisherman's young widow who is defeated by poverty and the elements.

Amor materno: Balada

¡Pobre Lisa!… Entristecida
y absorta, está contemplando
la mar embravecida
mientras la faz dolorida
van dos lágrimas surcando.

Tiene un niño
en sus brazos
que la mira
con amor.

¡Pobre madre!
¡¡Pobre niño!!
¿Adivina
su dolor?

Tal vez; que en sus labios rojos
no se advierte una sonrisa;
y tan sólo se divisa
hondo pesar en sus ojos…
¡Pobre niño! Pobre Lisa!

¡Pobre Lisa!
¡Y cuán bella!

A Mother's Love: Ballad

Poor Lisa! Sad and
forlorn she beholds
the enraged current
while two tears stream down
her grief-stricken face.

In her arms
a child who
looks at her
tenderly.

Poor mother!
Poor infant!
Does he guess
her sorrow?

Perhaps, for no smile
plays on his red lips;
and nothing but pain
reflects from his eyes.
Poor child! Poor Lisa!

Poor Lisa!
So lovely!

Atesoras
gracias mil.
¡¡Pobre niño!!
¡Cuán hermosa
es la cara
de marfil!

—Duerme, mi bien, y no llores,—
La triste madre cantó;
—Duerme, flor de mis amores;
borre el sueño tus dolores
ya que pan no tengo yo.

Esas ondas
sepultaron
a tu padre,
sin piedad;
y nos dieron
duelos, hambre
y orfandad.

¡Palideces, amor mío!
¡Mira, Dios santo, mi afán!
¡Piedad de mi duelo impío!
De hambre se muere y de frío…
¡Pan para mi hijo, pan!…

You possess
untold charms.
Poor infant!
How pretty
your face of
ivory.

"Sleep, my love, don't cry,"
the sad mother sang.
"Sleep, precious flower,
let sleep soothe your pain
since bread I have none.

"Merciless,
these waves took
your father
to his grave
and brought us
grief, hunger,
bereavement.

"You grow pale, my love!
God, see my anguish!
Pity my hardship!
He's dying of hunger.
Bread for my child, bread!"

Y la pobre
pescadera
en la arena
se postró;
y la espuma
de las olas
sus cabellos
salpicó.

En tanto, la marea veloz iba avanzando:
las nubes se agrupaban, silbaba el vendaval;
y, muerta casi, Lisa seguía sollozando
sin que se apercibiese del recio temporal.

Un trueno de repente llegó a sus oídos:
de espanto y pena yerta, la triste frente alzó;
entonces de las olas los cóncavos gemidos
con su hijo entre los brazos, inmóvil escuchó.

—La muerte, gritó Lisa: huyamos, hijo mío;
levanta, que en mis brazos, no te puedo salvar.
También yo siento el hambre, también me mata el frío;
Valor, hijo, o nos traga el encrespado mar.

And the poor
woman fell
to her knees
in the sand;
and the foam
of the waves
splashed her hair
with water.

The tide kept advancing rapidly,
the clouds gathered, the whirlwind whistled;
near death, Lisa did not stop weeping,
unaware of the tempest's fury.

A sudden thunderclap reached her ears;
rigid with fright, she raised her sad face;
listening to the sea's hollow moans,
she stood still with her child in her arms.

"Death," shouted Lisa. "Let's flee, my son.
Stand up, in my arms I can't save you,
I too am weak from hunger and cold.
Courage, or the sea will swallow us"

Ya no escuchaba el niño; exámine, espirante,
sobre el materno pecho su frente se dobló…
En vez de huir la triste, asióse a él delirante,
y en su irritado seno el mar los sepultó.

Flores

The child, breath fading, no longer heard,
his head inclined on his mother's breast.
Not fleeing, she clutched him in despair—
the vexed sea buried them in its lap.

Rosalía de Castro
(1837–85)
Rosalía de Castro Murguía

The Spanish title for *Cantares gallegos* (1863; "Galician Songs") may be an indication of Rosalía de Castro's hesitancy about publishing a collection of poems written entirely in a non-Castilian language. The book, which celebrates her region's popular customs, folklore, and traditions, was well received in Galicia and played a major role in the revival of Galician as a literary language. The poem "Quíxente tanto, meniña, ..." ("I loved you so, sweetie, . . .") is typical of the lighthearted and folksy tone that prevails in *Cantares gallegos*, but "Pasa, río, pasa, río, ..." ("Flow on, river, flow on . . .") anticipates the painful theme of emigration, which Castro explores more extensively in her next Galician volume, *Follas novas* (1880; "New Leaves"). The speaker in "¡Adiós!" ("Farewell!"), whose love of his native soil and his reluctance to depart are evident, suggests the plight of the men who were forced to emigrate because of poverty, and "Tecín soia a miña tea, ..." ("Alone I weave my cloth, . . .") illustrates the hardship of the women who were left to fend for themselves. Besides showing empathy for her countrymen, Castro expresses her own feelings of melancholy, loss, grief, and longing in *Follas novas*. The disheartened mood that permeates "Cada noite en chorando pensaba..." ("Every night I long, amid tears, . . .") grows even more somber in *En las orillas del Sar* (1884; "By the River Sar"), written in Castilian and published a year before her death.

During her lifetime, Castro's fame was limited, in part because she composed some of her finest poems in Galician. The poets of the Generation of '98, who noted echoes of their own existential anxiety in Castro's indefinable apprehensions, were among the first to appreciate her intimate lyricism, simple diction, and innovative prosody. Their view of Castro as one of the most outstanding poets of the nineteenth century is widely shared today.

"Quíxente tanto, meniña, ..."

"Quíxente tanto, meniña,
tívenche tan grande amor,
que para min eras lúa,
branca aurora e craro sol;
augua limpa en fresca fonte,
rosa do xardín de Dios,
alentiño do meu peito,
vida do meu corazón."
Así che falín un día,
camiñiño de San Lois,
todo oprimido de angustia,
todo ardente de pasión,
mentras que ti me escoitabas
depinicando unha frol,
porque eu non vise os teus ollos
que refrexaban traiciós.
Dempois que *si* me dixeches
en proba de teu amor
décheme un caraveliño
que gardín no corazón.
¡Negro caravel maldito,

"I loved you so, sweetie, . . ."

"I loved you so, sweetie,
great was my love for you,
for me you were the moon,
white dawn, and brilliant sun,
clear water in fresh fount,
a rose from God's garden,
the air that filled my lungs,
the life of my heart."
That's what I said one day
on the way to San Lois,
oppressed by anxiousness,
set aflame with passion.
While you listened to me,
you plucked a flower, so
I wouldn't see your eyes
sparkling with treachery.
After you told me *yes*
as proof of your love, you
gave me a carnation
that I kept near my heart.
Cursèd black carnation

que me fireu de dolor!
Mais a pasar polo río,
¡o caravel afondou!...
Tan bo camiño ti leves
como o caravel levou.

Obras, vol. 1

that wounded me with pain!

But I passed the river

and the carnation drowned! . . .

May your fate be the same

as the damned carnation's.

Pasa, río, pasa, río,...

Pasa, río, pasa, río,
co teu maino rebulir;
pasa, pasa antre as froliñas
color de ouro e de marfil,
a quen cos teus doces labios
tan doces cousas lles dis.
Pasa, pasa, mais non vexan
que te vas ao mar sin fin,
porque estonces, ¡ai, probiñas,
cánto choraran por ti!
¡Si souperas que estrañeza,
si souperas que sofrir
desque del vivo apartada
o meu corazón sentiu!
Tal me acoden as soidades,
tal me queren afrixir,
que inda máis feras me afogan,
si as quero botar de min.
I, ¡ai, que fora das froliñas
véndote lonxe de si
ir pola verde ribeira
da ribeira do Carril!

Flow on, river, flow on . . .

Flow on, river, flow on
with your gentle rumble;
flow amid the flowers—
golden and ivory—
and with your charming lips
whisper the sweetest things.
But don't let them see you
flow to the endless sea,
because the poor flowers
would surely cry for you!
If you knew the yearning,
if you knew the sorrow
my heart suffers now that
I must live without him!
Such longing seizes me
and holds me in its grip,
clasping more firmly when
I try to free myself.
Oh, what if the flowers
saw you so far from them
flowing on the green shores,
the shores of the Carril?

Pasa, pasa caladiño,
co teu maino rebulir,
camiño do mar salado,
camiño do mar sin fin;
e leva estas lagrimiñas,
si has de chegar por alí,
pretiño dos meus amores,
pretiño do meu vivir.
¡Ai, quen lágrimiña fora
pra ir, meu ben, unda ti!...
¡Quen fixera un camiñiño
para pasar, ai de min!

Si o mar tivera barandas,
fórate ver ao Brasil;
mais o mar non ten barandas,
amor meu, ¿por donde hei de ir?

Obras, vol. 2

Flow, quietly, flow on,
with your gentle rumble,
flow to the salty sea,
to the limitless sea;
carry along these tears
in case you arrive there
near the love of my heart,
near the love of my life.
If I could be a tear
to be near you, my love!
Oh, if only there were
a road I could travel!

If the sea had pathways,
I would go to Brazil,
but, my love, without them,
how am I to get there?

¡Adiós!

¡Adiós!, montes e prados, igrexas e campanas,
¡adiós!, Sar e Sarela, cubertos de enramada,
¡adiós!, Vidán alegre, moíños e hondanadas,
Conxo, o do craustro triste i as soedades prácidas,
San Lourenzo, o escondido, cal un niño antre as ramas,
Balvis, para min sempre o das fondas lembranzas,
Santo Domingo, en onde canto eu quixen descansa,
vidas da miña vida, anacos das entrañas.
E vós tamén, sombrisas paredes solitarias
que me vicheis chorare soia e desventurada,
¡adiós!, sombras queridas; ¡adiós!, sombras odiadas;
outra vez os vaivéns da fertuna
pra lonxe me arrastran.

Cando volver, se volvo, todo estará onde estaba:
os mesmos montes negros i as mesmas alboradas,
do Sar e do Sarela, mirándose nas auguas.
Os mesmos verdes campos, as mesmas torres pardas
da catedral severa, ollando as lontananzas.
Mais os que agora deixo, tal como a fonte mansa,
ou no verdor da vida, sin tempestás nin bágoas,
¡canto, cando eu tornare, vítimas da mudanza,
terán de présa andando na senda da desgracia!
I eu... mais eu nada temo no mundo,
¡que a morte me tarda!

Obras vol. 2

Farewell!

Farewell to mountains and meadows, churches and bells,
farewell, Sar and Sarela, blanketed with groves,
farewell cheery Vidán, with your mills and valleys,
Conxo, with your sad cloister and tranquillity,
San Lourenzo, hidden like a nest in the tree,
Balvis, for me a place of profound memories,
Santo Domingo, where I so wanted to rest,
lights of my life, fragments of my innermost being.
Farewell also to you, gloomy and lonesome walls
that have seen me shed tears in hapless solitude,
farewell, beloved shadows! Farewell, despised ones!
    Once more, fortune's vagaries
    draw me far away.

When I return, if I do, all will be unchanged;
the same black mountains and the same morning sunrise,
the Sar and Sarela reflecting each other.
The same verdant fields, the same brownish-gray towers
of the severe cathedral, scanning the distance.
But those I now leave behind are like the calm fount,
in the spring of their lives, without turmoil or tears,
how many, upon my return, will have hastened
toward the road of disaster, victims of change!
    And I . . . fear nothing on earth
    but my death's delay!

Rico ou probe, algún día...

Rico ou probe, algún día
¡con que contento e pracidez folgaba!
I agora, probe ou rico, ó desdichado
¡todo, todo lle falta!

En balde veñen días, pasan anos,
e inda sigros pasaran;
se hai abondosas fontes que se secan,
tamén as hai que eternamente manan;
mais as fontes perenes nesta vida
son sempre envenenadas.

Nelas o esprito que ofendido pena,
na humidá enferma do rencor se baña,
sin que dado lle sea
beber do olvido nas saudosas auguas.

¡Odio!, fillo do inferno,
pode acaba-lo amor, mais ti n'acabas,
mamoria que recorda-las ofensas.
Si, si, ¡de ti mal haia!

Obras, vol. 2

Rich or poor, one day . . .

Rich or poor, one day
he frolicked with such pleasure and joy!
And now, poor or rich, wretched fellow,
he has nothing left!

The days and years pass in vain, even
centuries may pass.
Some plentiful rivers diminish,
many others flow eternally,
but the rivers that endure in life
are always poisoned.

In them the aggrieved soul does penance,
bathed in resentment's damp bitterness,
unable to drink
the sweet waters of forgetfulness.

Hatred, child of hell!
Love may end, but you, memory that
remembers affronts, you never will.
Yes, yes, you be damned!

Cada noite eu chorando pensaba...

Cada noite eu chorando pensaba...
que esta noite tan grande non fora,
que durase... e durase antre tanto
    que a noite das penas
    me envolve loitosa.

Mais a luz insolente do día,
    costante e traidora,
    cada amañecida
penetraba radiante de groria
hastra o leito donde eu me tendera
    coas miñas congoxas.

Desde estonces busquei as tiniebras
    máis negras e fondas,
e busqueinas en vano, que sempre
trás da noite topaba ca aurora...
So en min mesma, buscando no oscuro
i entrando na sombra,
vin a noite que nunca se acaba
na miña alma soia.

Obras, vol. 2

Every night I long, amid tears, . . .

Every night I long, amid tears,
for this long night never to end,
but to last . . . and last as long as
    the night of my pains
    that shrouds me sadly.

But insolent daylight, guileful
    and ever-present,
    each early morning
makes its way, radiant with glory,
to the bed where I lie stretched out
    in my agony.

Since then I search for the blackest
    and deepest darkness
but I search for it in vain, since
after every night I find dawn . . .
Only when I search within me
    amid my shadows,
I see that the night without end
    is in my own soul.

¿Quen non xime?

Luz e progreso en todas partes..., pero
as dudas nos corazós,
e bágoas que un non sabe por que corren,
e dores que un non sabe por que son.

Outro cantar, din, cansados
deste estribilo, os que chegando van
nunha nova fornada, e que andan cegos
buscando o que índa non hai.

¡Réprobos!... Sempre ó oculto perguntando
que, mudo, nada vos di.
Buscade a fe, que se perdeu na duda,
e deixade de xemir.

Mais eles tamén perdidos
por unha i outra senda van e vén
sin que sepan, ¡coitados!, por onde andan
sin paz, sin rumbo e sin fe.

. . . .

Triste é o cantar que cantamos,
mais ¿que facer se outro melhor non hai?
moita luz deslumbra os ollos,
causa inquietude o moito desear.
Cando unha peste arrebata

Who Does Not Lament?

Light and progress all around . . . but doubts
    in our hearts, and tears
that flow without any known reason,
and sorrows whose causes are unknown.

    A different song,
say those tired of the same refrain,
the new crowd searching blindly for what
    does not exist yet.

Sinners! You consult the occult but
    receive no answer.
Search for the faith that was lost in doubt,
    and stop lamenting.

    But they too are lost,
walking back and forth, without knowing,
poor things, where they're going, with no peace,
faith, or direction.
. . . .

    We sing a sad song
but what if there is no better one?
    Too much light dazzles,
too much desire causes anxiousness.
    If a pest slays men,

homes tras homes, n' hai máis
que enterrar de présa os mortos,
baixala frente, e esperar
que pasen as correntes apestadas...
¡Que pasen..., que outras vendrán!

Obras, vol. 2

one by one, we must
bury the dead fast,
bow our heads and wait
for these pestilent currents to pass . . .
But others will come!

O pazo de A***

Era ó caer da tarde,
encomenzaba o cántico dos grilos,
xorda a presa ruxía,
brilaban lonxe os lumes fuxitivos.

Ó pe do monte, maxestuoso erguíase
na aldea escura o caserón querido,
ca oliva centenaria
de cortinax ó ventanil servindo.

Deserta a escalinata,
soio o paterno niño,
e enriba del caendo misteriosas
coas sombras do crepúsculo, as do olvido.

¿Quen ó pasado volve
os ollos compasivos?
¿Quen se lembra dos mortos
se inda non poden recordarse os vivos?

Obras, vol. 2

The Manor House of A***

It was late afternoon,
the crickets embarked on their chant,
the sea wall groaned faintly,
unsteady lights flickered far off.

At the mountain's foot, loftily
rising from the dark village, stood
the dear house, an ancient
olive tree shading its window.

The entrance stands empty
to the ancestral nest,
on which mysterious shadows
of twilight and oblivion fall.

Who reflects on the past
with compassionate eyes?
Who remembers the dead
if the living are forgotten?

Estranxeira na súa patria

Na xa vella baranda
entapizada de hedras e de lirios
foise a sentar calada e tristemente
frente do tempro antiguo.

Interminable procesión de mortos,
uns en corpo no-máis, outros no esprito,
veu pouco a pouco aparecer na altura
do direito camiño,
que monótono e branco relumbraba
tal como un lenzo nun herbal tendido.

Contempróu cal pasaban e pasaban
correndo hacia o infinito,
sin que ó fixaren nela
os ollos apagados e afundidos
deran sinal nin moestra
de habela nalgún tempo conocido.
I uns eran seus amantes noutros días,
deudos eran os máis i outros amigos,
compañeiros da infancia,
sirventes e veciños.

A Stranger in Her Homeland

On the old terrace,
embroidered with ivy and lilies,
she reclined in silence and sadness,
facing the temple.

An endless procession of the dead,
some in body, others in spirit,
came into view gradually from
farther up the road,
which glowed with monotonous whiteness
like a canvas spread out on the grass.

She watched them as they passed by, rushing
to infinity,
not glancing at her
with their sunken and dull eyes, giving
no signal or sign
of having known her once in the past.
At one time, some had been her lovers,
many others, relatives or friends,
childhood companions,
servants and neighbors.

Mais pasando e pasando, diante dela
fono os mortos aqueles prosiguiendo
    a indiferente marcha,
    camiño do infinito,
mentras cerraba a noite silenciosa
    os seus loitos tristísimos
entorno da estranxeira na súa patria,
    que, sin lar ni arrimo,
sentada na baranda contempraba
cal brilaban os lumes fuxitivos.

Obras, vol. 1

But the dead continued to pass by
in front of her, proceeding with their
    indifferent march
    to infinity,
while night, descending without a sound,
    enveloped in sad
mourning the stranger in her homeland,
    who, without a home
or protection, sat on the terrace
gazing at the glow of furtive lights.

Tecín soia a miña tea,...

Tecín soia a miña tea,
sembrei soia o meu nabal,
soia vou por leña ó monte,
soia a vexo arder no lar.
Nin na fonte nin no prado,
así morra coa carrax,
el no ha de virme a erguer,
el xa non me pousará.
¡Que tristeza! O vento soa,
canto o grilo ó seu compás...
Ferbe o pote... mais, meu caldo,
soíña te he de cear.
Cala, rula, os teus arrulos,
ganas de morrer me dan;
cala, grilo, que si cantas
sinto negras soidás.
O meu homiño perdeuse,
ninguén sabe en onde vai...
Anduriña que pasache
con el as ondas do mar,
anduriña, voa, voa,
ven e dime en onde está.

Obras, vol. 1

Alone I weave my cloth, . . .

Alone I weave my cloth,
alone I plant turnips,
alone I look for wood,
alone I watch it burn.
Though I blaze with fury,
he won't be in the field
or by the fount to ease
or unload my burden.
How sad! The wind thunders,
the cricket plays its tune . . .
the pot boils . . . but, dear soup,
I'll sup alone with you.
Hush, turtledove, when you
coo I feel like dying;
hush, cricket, for your song
fills me with dark yearning.
My man is lost, no one
knows where he's wandering . . .
Swallow, who crossed the waves
of the sea with him, fly,
swallow, fly, then return
to tell me where he is.

Sempre pola morte esperas,...

Sempre pola morte esperas,
mais a morte nunca vén;
¡coitado!, pensas que as penas
poden matar dunha vez?
Nunca, que son coma o hético;
tras de roer e roer,
só deixan un corpo cando
xa non tén que comer nel.
Cando a iaugua das penas
se reverte na copa sin medida,
soio é remedio a morte
para curar da vida.

Obras, vol. 1

Always waiting for death, . . .

Always waiting for death,
but death does not arrive.
You poor thing! Did you think
that pain kills completely?
Never. Like consumption
it gnaws and gnaws, leaving
the body only when
there is no more to eat.
When a bottomless cup
overflows with sorrow,
the only remedy
that can cure life is death.

¿Por que?

—¡Escoita! Os algoasiles
andan correndo a aldea;
mais, ¿como pagar, como, si un non pode
inda paga-la renda?

Embargarannos todo, que no teñen
esas xentes concencia, ni ten alma.
¡Quedaremos por portas,
meus fillos das entrañas!

¡Mala muerte vos mate
antes de que aquí entredes!...
Dos probes, ó sentirvos,
os corazós, ¡cal baten tristemente!

—María, se non fora
porque hai un Dios que premia e que castiga
eu matara eses homes
como mata un raposo a unha galiña.

—¡Silencio! ¡Non brasfemes,
que este é un valle de lágrimas!...
Mais ¿por que a algúns lles toca sufrir tanto
i outros a vida antre contentos pasan?

Obras, vol. 1

Why?

"Listen! The bailiffs
roam the village;
but how can we pay them if we can't
even pay the rent?

"They will confiscate everything, for
these men have neither soul nor conscience.
My dearest children,
we will be thrown out!

"May you be struck dead
before you enter!
When the poor hear you,
how sadly their hearts begin to beat."

"María, but for
a God who punishes and rewards,
I would kill these men
exactly as a fox kills a hen."

"Quiet. Don't blaspheme,
'tis a vale of tears!
But why are some fated to suffer
so much while others live happily?"

Tan soio

Os dous da terra lonxe
andamos e sufrimos, ¡ai de min!
Mais ti tan soio te recordas dela,
i eu, dela e máis de ti.

Ambos errantes polo mundo andamos
i as nosas forzas acabando van,
mas, ¡ai!, ti nela atoparás descanso
i eu tan soio na morte o hei de atopar.

Obras, vol. 1

Only

Both of us have traveled
far from our land, and how we suffer
But while you long only for your land,
I long for my land and you.

Both of us wander, lost in the world,
and our strength is beginning to ebb,
but, oh, you will encounter some rest,
and I will encounter only death.

Era la última noche,...

Era la última noche,
la noche de las tristes despedidas,
y apenas si una lágrima empañaba
sus serenas pupilas.
Como el criado que deja
al amo que le hostiga,
arreglando su hatillo, murmuraba
casi con la emoción de la alegría:

—Llorar! ¿por qué? Fortuna es que podamos
abandonar nuestras humildes tierras;
el duro pan que nos negó la patria,
por más que los extraños nos maltraten,
no ha de faltarnos en la patria ajena.

Y los hijos contentos se sonríen,
y la esposa, aunque triste, se consuela
con la firme esperanza
de que el que parte ha de volver por ella.

Pensar que han de partir, ése es el sueño
que da fuerza en su angustia a los que quedan;
¡cuánto en ti pueden padecer, oh patria,
si ya tus hijos sin dolor te dejan!

Obras, vol. 1

It was the last night, . . .

It was the last night,
the sad night of sorrowful good-byes,
and barely a single tear moistened
his serene pupils.
Like the servant who
leaves a harsh master,
he whispered while tying his bundle
with an emotion resembling joy:

"Why should I cry? It's fortunate that
we can abandon our humble lands.
The hard bread our homeland denies us
will be ours in foreign lands, even
if the strangers do not treat us well."

And the children smile with contentment
and the wife, though sad, consoles herself
with the steady hope
that her husband will come back for her.

They too will depart: this dream eases
the worries of those who stay behind.
Homeland, how your children must suffer,
if they can leave you without regret!

Del mar azul las transparentes olas...

Del mar azul las transparentes olas
    mientras blandas murmuran
sobre la arena, hasta mis pies rodando,
tentadoras me besan y me buscan.

Inquietas lamen de mi planta el borde,
lánzanme airosas su nevada espuma,
y pienso que me llaman, que me atraen
    hacia sus salas húmedas.

    Mas cuando ansiosa quiero
seguirlas por la líquida llanura,
se hunde mi pie en la linfa transparente
    y ellas de mí se burlan.

Y huyen abandonándome en la playa
a la terrena, inacabable lucha,
como en las tristes playas de la vida
me abandonó inconstante la fortuna.

Obras, vol. 1

The transparent waves of the blue sea, . . .

The transparent waves of the blue sea,
    murmuring softly
on the sand as they roll to my feet,
look for me and kiss me temptingly.

Restlessly they lap against my toes,
haughtily splashing their snowy foam,
and I think they are inviting me
    to their dampened halls.

    But when I wish to
follow them across the liquid field,
my feet sink in the crystal water
    and the waves mock me.

And they flee, stranding me on the beach
of an earthly struggle without end,
just as fortune's inconstancies have
abandoned me on life's sad shore.

Ansia que ardiente crece,...

Ansia que ardiente crece,
vertiginoso vuelo,
tras de algo que nos llama
con murmurar incierto,
sorpresas celestiales,
dichas que nos asombran;
así cuando buscamos lo escondido,
así comienzan del amor las horas.

Inaplacable angustia,
hondo dolor del alma,
recuerdo que no muere,
deseo que no acaba,
vigilia de la noche,
torpe sueño del día,
es lo que queda del placer gustado,
es el fruto podrido de la vida.

Obras, vol. 1

Anxiousness burning bright, . . .

Anxiousness burning bright,
dizzy flight in pursuit
of something calling us
with shadowy whispers,
heavenly surprises,
perplexing happiness;
this is when we search for the hidden,
this is when the hours of love begin.

Relentless agony,
the soul's profound sorrow,
undying memory,
desire that never ends,
nocturnal vigilance,
disturbing daytime sleep;
all that remains after the taste of
pleasure is the putrid fruit of life.

De este mundo en la comedia...

De este mundo en la comedia
eterna, vienen y van
bajo un mismo velo envueltas
la mentira y la verdad;
por eso al verlas el hombre
tras del mágico cendal
que vela la faz de entrambas,
nunca puede adivinar
con certeza cuál es de ellas
la mentira o la verdad.

Obras, vol. 1

In this world's eternal . . .

In this world's eternal
comedy, falsehood and
truth come and go, hidden
beneath the selfsame veil.
Thus, seeing their faces
behind the magic cloth,
no one can ever guess
with complete certainty
which of the two is false
and which of the two, true.

Sed de amores tenía, y dejaste...

Sed de amores tenía, y dejaste
que la apagase en tu boca,
¡piadosa samaritana!,
y te encontraste sin honra,
ignorando que hay labios que secan
y que manchan cuanto tocan.

¡Lo ignorabas... y ahora lo sabes!
Pero yo sé también, pecadora
compasiva, porque a veces
hay compasiones traidoras,
que si el sediento volviese
a implorar misericordia,
su sed de nuevo apagaras,
samaritana piadosa.

No volverá, te lo juro;
desde que una fuente enlodan
con su pico esas aves de paso,
se van a beber a otra.

Obras, vol. 1

He felt a thirst for love, and you allowed . . .

He felt a thirst for love, and you allowed
him to quench it with your lips,
merciful Samaritan,
and thus you lost your honor,
not realizing that some lips parch and
disgrace everything they touch.

You were unaware . . . and now you know it!
But I also know, kindhearted sinner,
that some acts of charity
are treacherous, and that if
he returned to implore you
for forgiveness one more time,
you would quench his thirst anew,
merciful Samaritan.

He will not return, I swear,
for after their beaks muddy
a fount, these birds of passage
seek to drink from other springs.

Glorias hay que deslumbran, cual deslumbra...

Glorias hay que deslumbran, cual deslumbra
el vivo resplandor de los relámpagos,
y que como él se apagan en la sombra,
sin dejar de su luz huella ni rastro.

Yo prefiero a ese brillo de un instante,
la triste soledad donde batallo,
y donde nunca a perturbar mi espíritu
llega el vano rumor de los aplausos.

Obras, vol. 1

There are glories that bedazzle us . . .

There are glories that bedazzle us
like the blinding brilliance of lightning,
and they too are snuffed out in the dark,
not leaving any trace of their light.

Rather than this brief glare, I prefer
the sad solitude where I battle
and where the vain echo of applause
never comes to perturb my spirit.

¡Oh gloria!, deidad vana cual todas las deidades...

¡Oh gloria!, deidad vana cual todas las deidades
que en el orgullo humano tienen altar y asiento,
jamás te rendí culto, jamás mi frente altiva
se inclinó de tu trono ante el dosel soberbio.

En el dintel oscuro de mi pobre morada,
no espero que detengas el breve alado pie;
porque jamás mi alma te persiguió en sus sueños,
ni de tu amor voluble quiso gustar la miel.

¡Cuántos te han alcanzado que no te merecían,
y cuántos cuyos nombres debiste hacer eterno,
en brazos del olvido más triste y más profundo
perdidos para siempre duermen el postrer sueño!

Obras, vol. 1

O glory! Goddess, vain like every deity, . . .

O glory! Goddess, vain like every deity,
seated on the altar of human vanity,
I never worshipped you, or reverently bowed
my proud head before your throne's regal canopy.

I do not expect you to set your wingèd foot
on the gloomy threshold of my modest dwelling,
because my soul never pursued you in her dreams,
nor did she wish to taste the nectar of your love.

How many have attained you undeservingly
and how many whose names should ring eternally
sleep their last sleep embraced by the most profound
and sorrowful oblivion, forgotten forever!

Sintióse agonizar, mil y mil veces,...

Sintióse agonizar, mil y mil veces,
de dolor, de vergüenza y de amargura,
mas aunque tantas tras de tantas fueron
    no se murió ninguna.

    Embargada de asombro
al ver la resistencia de su vida,
en sus horas sin término pensaba,
llena de horror, si nunca moriría.

Pero una voz secreta y misteriosa
la dijo un día con acento extraño:
Hasta el momento de tocar la dicha
no se mueren jamás los desdichados.

Obras, vol. 1

She felt a thousand agonies, . . .

She felt a thousand agonies,
of sorrow, shame, and bitterness;
although they followed each other,
    not one of them died.

    Seized with amazement
to behold her life's resistance,
in her endless hours she wondered
in horror if she'd ever die.

One day a strange and secret voice
told her in an unusual tone:
Not until they have tasted joy
do those who are unhappy die.

Victorina Sáenz de Tejada
(1841–?)

Pseudonyms: Sor María de los Ángeles, Una Hija de María, Una Religiosa del Convento de Sancti Spiritus de Sevilla

Victorina Sáenz de Tejada was still very young when her father, a field marshal, died in Cuba. His death left the family in penury, and Saénz de Tejada moved from the city of Granada to the provincial town of Antequera, where she supported herself by sewing. At the same time, she began writing poetry, achieving local fame at age thirteen with her poem "A Jesús crucificado" ("To Christ on the Cross"). About a decade later, the literary circles of Antequera helped finance the publication of her collected poems, *Poesías* (1865). When she moved to Sevilla in 1869, she contributed her writings to such Catholic publications as *La verdad Católica* and *Las hijas del sol*. In 1876, she entered the convent of Espíritu Santo, taking the name of Sister María de los Ángeles. After professing her vows, she continued to write poems and plays, signing her work with various religious pseudonyms. Her poem "La inconstancia" ("Fickleness") depicts fickleness as a force capable of destroying the most idyllic existence.

La inconstancia

Infeliz corazón, rico en amores:
cuando irradiando luz nueva existencia
te ofrece la risueña adolescencia,
en ti sientes brotar cándidas flores.

Las baña con sus rayos bienhechores
el sol de la esperanza, y la inocencia
a sus cálices da fragrante esencia,
y a sus hojas suavísimas colores.

Ellas transforman nuestro pobre suelo
en el edén más bello de ternura;
mas cuando el alma goza todo un cielo

y extasiada contempla la hermosura
de estas flores de célica fragrancia
las viene a marchitar, ¡ay!, la *inconstancia*.

Poesías

Fickleness

Hapless heart, rich in loves: when glowing
and cheerful adolescence renews
your existence, you sense the budding
of unblemished flowers within you.

Radiant hope bathes them with soothing
rays, and innocence bestows fragrant
aromas to their calyxes and
colors their petals with soft-hued tones.

They transform our sterile soil into
a pleasant Eden of tenderness;
but when the soul enjoys heavenly

bliss and contemplates in ecstasy
the beauty of these fragrant flowers,
fickleness comes and, oh, withers them.

Eladia Bautista y Patier

When Eladia Bautista y Patier was still an adolescent, her parents and two sisters died, leaving her in charge of three younger sisters. Despite these personal hardships, she pursued her literary interests and took part in poetry contests. Her participation in one of the contests sponsored by the Sociedad Abolicionìsta Española ("Spanish Abolitionist Society") greatly impressed Faustina Sáez de Melgar, who encouraged the publication of Bautista y Patier's collected poems (1870) and even contributed the prologue. In 1882, Bautista y Patier's last known poems appeared in *París Charmant-Artistique,* a magazine edited by Sáez de Melgar. In the poem featured here, "A un pájaro" ("To a Bird"), the speaker envies a bird's unfettered flight and contrasts it with the lack of freedom that she suggests is a part of the feminine condition.

A un pájaro

Cruza libre los espacios,
luce en el viento tus galas,
ya que Dios para ser libre
ha querido que tú nazcas.

¡Ojalá que el alma mía
te llevases en tus alas,
que vive cautiva y triste
vertiendo ardorosas lágrimas!

Goza de tiernos amores,
tu dicha inefable canta,
que tú naciste avecilla,
y yo mujer desgraciada.

Poesías

To a Bird

Fly freely across space,
displaying your plumage
in the wind, since God wished
for you to be born free.

If only on your wings
you could carry my soul
that lives sadly confined,
shedding passionate tears.

Savor your tender loves,
sing of your boundless bliss:
for you were born a bird—
I, a wretched woman.

Patrocinio de Biedma

(1858–1927)

Patrocinio de Biedma y la Moneda
Anagrammatic pseudonym: Ticiano Imab

Throughout her life, Patrocinio de Biedma suffered the loss of loved ones. Not surprisingly, death was a recurrent theme in much of her poetry, and it is the subject of her poem "La muerte" ("Death"), featured here. Born to an aristocratic Sevillian family, she was married at age fifteen and widowed ten years later. All three children from that marriage died at a young age, and the loss of her oldest son prompted her to write the poems that are collected in *Guirnalda de pensamientos* (1872; "A Garland of Thoughts"). Her second poetic volume, *Recuerdos de un ángel* (1876; "Memories of an Angel"), was dedicated to her youngest son, José, who died when he was six. Biedma founded and directed the magazine *Cádiz,* named after the city where she established her residence after 1877. The topics that continued to interest her, and to which she devoted numerous novels, short stories, and journal articles, were children, feminism, and pacifism.

La muerte

No hay nada que redima de la muerte
ni que domine su horrible encanto;
siembra doquier desolación y espanto
y es temida del débil y del fuerte.

Al solo impulso de su mano inerte
rompe los lazos del amor más santo,
y al disolver el corazón en llanto
sobre la vida su amargura vierte.

Todo lo vence: cuanto existe y nace
se rinde a su dominio, a su fiereza
que en polvo vano su poder deshace,

ella abate el valor, la fortaleza,
sólo al alma, que el soplo de Dios hace,
arrebatar no puede su grandeza.

Guirnalda

Death

Nothing can deliver us from Death
or tame his terrible enchantment;
he sows desolation and despair
and is feared by the weak and the strong.

With a mere flick of his rigid hand
he breaks the most sacred bonds of love,
and hearts thus emptied from their weeping
pour down streams of bitterness on life.

He conquers everything; all that lives
surrenders to his ferocious might,
which reduces their power to dust.

He triumphs over strength and valor,
but he cannot vanquish the grandeur
of the soul created with God's breath.

Rosario de Acuña
(1851–1923)
Rosario de Acuña Villanueva de la Iglesia
Pseudonym: Remigio Andrés Delafón

Rosario de Acuña was of aristocratic lineage, although she never used her title of countess of Acuña. She was schooled by nuns, but her poor vision prevented her from completing her formal studies, and she attributed much of her education to travels in Italy, France, and Portugal. At age twenty-five, she premiered her highly successful play, *Rienzi el Tribuno* (inspired, like Wagner's opera *Rienzi, the Last of the Tribunes*, by Edward Bulwer-Lytton's novel), becoming the second woman in nineteenth-century Spain—after Gertrudis Gómez de Avellaneda—to stage a theatrical work. After the publication that same year of Acuña's only collection of poems, *Ecos del alma* (1876; "Echoes of the Soul") Acuña dedicated herself mostly to drama, short stories, and essays. Also in 1876, she married Rafael de la Iglesia, but she left him after discovering his infidelity.

Acuña was the first woman to address Madrid's Ateneo when she gave a poetry recital at the venerable all-male institution in 1884. A freethinker and a member of a Freemason lodge, she provoked controversy and suffered persecution for her progressive and anticlerical ideas, as well as for her outspoken criticism of every type of social inequity. Like Carolina Coronado and Rosalía de Castro, among others, Acuña rejected "poetess" as a pejorative designator, and in the poem "¡Poetisa… !" she vows to tear up her poems in protest if anyone should call her by that name.

¡Triste destino!

Llega la vida a la vejez cansada
de un ayer solitario y aterido
y ante el recuerdo del dolor sufrido,
se anubla con el llanto la mirada;

el presente es llanura desolada,
y el porvenir la muerte y el olvido…
¡Cuán dura y triste la jornada ha sido
de soledad y pena acompañada!

¡Ebria de vicios, de odio y vanidades,
pasa feliz la imbécil muchedumbre
mirando siempre, como bestia, al suelo;

y camina a través de las edades,
sufriendo del dolor la pesadumbre,
alma que adora la virtud y el cielo!

Safo en Castilla (ed. Vázquez de Aldana)

Sad Destiny!

Life reaches old age exhausted from
a lonely and numbing yesterday,
and the remembrance of suffering
beclouds our vision with misty tears.

The present is a desolate plain
and the future, death and oblivion . . .
What a sad and difficult journey,
attended by loneliness and pain!

Drunk with vice, hatred, and vanity,
the dumb crowd passes by happily,
always gazing, like beasts, at the ground,

while the soul, worshipping virtue and
heaven, marches across the ages,
enduring the weight of affliction!

¡Poetisa... !

Raro capricho la mente sueña,
será inmodesta, vana aprensión.
  Tal palabra
  no me cuadra;
  su sonido
  a mi oído
  no murmura
  con dulzura
  de canción;
  no le presta
  armonía
  melodía
  y hace daño
  al corazón.

¿Tiemblo escucharla; será manía?
Oigo un murmullo cerca de mí:
  no me cuadra
  tal palabra;
  que el murmullo
  que al arrullo
  de la sátira
  nació,
  me lastima
  con su giro

Poetess!

The mind deceives us with strange caprices,
conceited and futile apprehensions.
  Such a name
  upsets me;
  its ringing
  in my ear
  is without
  the sweet sound
  of a song;
  harmony
  lends it no
  melody;
  instead, it
  wounds my heart.

I tremble at its name; am I obsessed?
I hear the murmurings all around me.
  Such a name
  upsets me;
  this mumble,
  arising
  from cooing
  ridicule,
  stings with its
  turn of phrase,

y un suspiro
me arrancó.

Si han de ponerme nombre tan feo
todos mis versos he de romper;
no me cuadra
tal palabra,
no la quiero;
yo prefiero
que a mi acento
lleve el viento,
y cual sombra
que se aleja
y no deja ni señal,
a mi canto,
que es mi llanto
arrebate
el vendaval.

Ecos

and wrests a
sigh from me.

If they call me by such an ugly name,
I will tear up all that I have written.
Such a name
upsets me;
I hate it;
I'd rather
have the wind
carry my
song like a
shadow that
leaves no trace
and my chants,
which are tears,
be swept up
in a gale.

Concepción Estevarena
(1854–76)
Rafaela María de la Concepción Ana de la Santísima Trinidad Estevarena y Gallardo

Having lost her mother to cholera when she was an infant, Concepción Estevarena spent her life taking care of her father. He forbade her to write poetry, but she disobeyed his wishes. Tragically, she died of tuberculosis at twenty-two, a year after her father's death. Her collected poems were published posthumously as *Últimas flores* (1876; "Last Flowers"), and in their intense brevity and their focus on sorrow, solitude, and suffering, they recall the verses of another native of Seville, Gustavo Adolfo Bécquer's *Rimas*. In her poem "Enigma," Estevarena examines some of her favorite subjects—the creative process, the passage of time, and death—and she seems to be carrying on a dialogue with Bécquer concerning the characteristics of a perfect artistic creation.

Enigma

Con todos los rumores que, mezclados,
    suben a lo infinito,
ha querido formar el hombre, ansioso,
de libertad el sacrosanto himno.

Notas, murmullos, huracanes, risas,
    palabras y suspiros,
nada es bastante; el himno deseado
siempre incompleto resonó en mi oído.

Mientras me lleve por el mar del mundo
    la nave del martirio,
no espero a escucharlo; falta un eco
universal, espléndido y divino.

Tal vez la eternidad es solamente
    quien guarda ese sonido,
y el velo de la muerte cubre el arpa
donde resuena el suspirado himno.

Últimas flores

Enigma

With all the mixed murmurs that rise up
  to infinity,
man has eagerly hoped to compose
the most hallowed hymn of liberty.

Notes, whisperings, hurricanes, laughter,
  words, and sighs—nothing
suffices; to my ears, the desired
hymn has always sounded incomplete.

While martyrdom's ship carries me on
  the sea of this world,
I shall never hear it; an echo,
divine, grand, and total, is needed.

Perhaps eternity is the sole
  guardian of this sound,
and the veil of death covers the harp
where the long-awaited hymn resounds.

Hojas y seres

Hojas que brotan en la misma rama,
si unas el viento logra arrebatar
y otras se quedan a la rama unidas,
¿a verse volverán?

Seres unidos por amantes lazos,
si los viene la muerte a separar
y unos se van mientras los otros quedan
¿a verse volverán?

Últimas flores

La pluma del genio

Fulguraba una luz junto a una pluma,
a que daba un matiz rojo y azul,
y, moviendo a las dos mi fantasía,
pensé que abandonaban su quietud;
y que, al tocarse ya, la pluma dijo:
—Las dos vertemos luz.
Y que la llama murmuraba entonces:
—No muere, como yo, la que das tú.

Últimas flores

Leaves

If the wind tears away some of
the leaves that bud on the same branch,
while others still cling to the bough
    will they meet again?

If death should rend apart beings
who have been united by love,
and some go, while others remain,
    will they meet again?

The Brilliant Pen

A light flickering near a pen
shaded it with red and blue hues.
In my fantasy, the two moved,
abandoning their quietness,
and, about to touch, the pen said,
"We both emit a glow,"
and the flame whispered in reply,
"But yours, unlike mine, will not die."

Una hora

En ti a la tierra venimos
en ti la vida dejamos;
eres breve si gozamos
y larga cuando sufrimos,
que siempre a los que sentimos
tus pasos iguales son;
basta una hora de aflicción
para encanecer a un hombre;
para eternizar un nombre
una hora de inspiración.

Últimas flores

An Hour

In you, we come to earth,
in you, we leave our lives;
you pass swiftly in joy
but last long in sorrow;
to those who feel the pace,
your tempo seems the same;
an hour of affliction
can whiten a man's hair;
an hour's inspiration,
immortalize a name.

Josefa Ugarte Barrientos
(1854–91)
Condesa Josefa Ugarte Barrientos de Parcent

In *Recuerdos de Andalucía* (1874; "Memories of Andalusia"), Josefa Ugarte Barrientos, known familiarly as Pepita Barrientos in her native Málaga, retold medieval stories and traditional legends in verse form. She continued writing poetry after her marriage to the count of Parcent and published her second volume, *Páginas en verso* ("Pages in Verse"), in 1882. After her death at the age of thirty-seven, her son edited her third volume, *Poesías selectas* (1904; "Selected Poems"). Her sonnet "Saffo" ("Sappho"), like Carolina Coronado's "El salto de Leucades" ("Leucadia"), describes the Greek poet's fatal leap in despair over her unrequited love for Phaon, but Ugarte Barrientos's poem emphasizes Sappho's poetic talent and the immutability of her verses.

Saffo

Sobre alta roca, desceñido el manto,
los ojos fijos en el claro cielo,
rota la lira sobre el duro suelo,
doliente exhala su postrero canto.

Absortas de su voz por el encanto,
gimen las musas en amargo duelo;
y vierte Saffo con febril anhelo
triste rauda de inspiración y llanto.

Llora de amor; el fuego que la inflama
el piélago no apaga, que se extiende
sobre sus miembros, e iracundo brama;

su noble acento las edades hiende;
que es poco el mar para extinguir la llama
que genio nombran, y que Dios enciende.

Poesías

Sappho

Standing on a high rock, with her robe
unfurled, her eyes fixed on the clear sky,
and her broken lyre on the hard ground,
she sings her last song in agony.

Enchanted by her enthralling voice,
the Muses lament in bitter grief,
and Sappho, with feverish longing,
pours out her inspiration and tears.

Love makes her weep; she burns with a fire
that not even the thunderous sea
covering her limbs can extinguish.

Her majestic chant rends the ages,
and the waters of the sea cannot
quell the flame called genius, lit by God.

Sofía Casanova

(1862–1958)

Sofía Pérez Casanova de Lutoslawski

This remarkable Galician poet, novelist, playwright, essayist, translator, and journalist married a Polish nobleman and later became one of the first female foreign correspondents during World War I and the Russian Revolution. Although fluent in Galician, Sofía Casanova seldom wrote in that language, publishing mostly in Spanish but also in Polish. After separating from her husband, she supported herself by writing essays and fiction and by contributing newspaper articles to *ABC*, one of Spain's leading conservative newspapers. The numerous honors bestowed on her include membership in Galicia's Royal Academy (particularly exceptional for a woman), the Great Cross of Alfonso XII, and a nomination for the Nobel Prize in Literature. As can be seen in her poem "Anhelo" ("Yearning"), Casanova shared a love and longing for her native region with Rosalía de Castro, a poet she greatly admired.

Anhelo

Seguid la carretera que tendida
entre prados está
como inmenso reptil de fina escama
parado a descansar,

y una plaza, antesala de una aldea,
por fin encontraréis
donde la vieja iglesia está orgullosa
de su misma vejez.

Y allí donde agrupadas las acacias
al declinar el sol
parecen los guardianes que se estrechan
para velar mejor;

allí donde las brumas misteriosas
flotan entre la luz;
donde corta el escueto campanario
el horizonte azul;

allí donde las negras cordilleras
parecen a mi afán

Yearning

Follow the highway that stretches out
  between meadows
like a giant reptile with fine scales,
  resting idly,

and there in the square—a vestibule
  to the village—
you will encounter an ancient church,
  proud of its age.

There where acacias crowd together
  in the sunset,
resembling guards who crane their necks to
  hold watch better;

there where mists drift mysteriously in
  and out of light;
where the plain belfry stands out against
  the blue skyline;

where, in my longing, the black mountains
  appear to me

negras perlas formando de los valles
    el sombrío collar,

está la pobre aldea que idolatro
    porque en ella nací,
cuando el otoño descolora impío
    de la selva el matiz.

Mi hogar perdido en la olvidada aldea
    contemplad con amor
y en su iglesia rezad, que allí he rezado
    mi primera oración.

¡Mi aldea! Quiero verla, quiero sola
    sus playas recorrer
y aspirar en sus auras nueva vida,
    la vida de la fe.

¡Llevádme, por favor! busco armonías
    que sólo encuentro allí,
secreto de sus noches y sus olas
    que cantan al gemir.

Quiero, Galicia, en tu adorado seno
    mi tristeza cantar,

like black pearls forming the dark necklace
    of the valleys;

there is the poor village I adore,
    where I was born
when impish autumn robbed the forest
    of its colors.

In the village, take a loving look
    at my lost home
and worship in the same church where I
    said my first prayer.

My village! I yearn to see it and
    roam its beaches,
breathe in a new life from its breezes,
    the life of faith.

Take me there! I search for harmonies
    found nowhere else,
the secret sound of nights and waves that
    sing their lament.

Galicia, in your lap I long to
    sing my sad song,

tú, que vives cual yo, desventurada,
    tú me comprenderás.

Quiero en tus soledades dar al mundo
    mi postrimer adiós…
y en tu iglesia rezar entre mis lágrimas
    mi postrera oración.

Poesías

for you, as forsaken as I, will
    understand me.

In your seclusion, I want to bid
    the world good-bye,
and in your church recite, amid tears,
    my final prayer.

Blanca de los Ríos

(1862–1956)

Blanca de los Ríos Nostench de Lampérez
Anagrammatic pseudonym: Carolina del Boss

An aristocrat and devout Catholic like her good friend Sofía Casanova, Blanca de los Ríos was a poet, novelist, journalist, and influential literary scholar. She wrote about the life and works of Teresa of Ávila, and she was praised by the Spanish Royal Academy for her important work on the Golden Age dramatist Tirso de Molina. Nevertheless, given the academy's policy (until 1978) not to admit women, Blanca de los Ríos's candidacy for membership was rejected. In 1911, she founded and directed the conservative magazine *Raza española*, and after her husband's death in 1923 she played an active role in literary events and institutions.

Her description of the artistic process in "Hoja blanca" ("Blank Page") as an arduous battle is in tune with turn-of-the-century sentiment and in contrast with the view of an earlier generation of feminine poets, who saw creation as a spontaneous, exuberant, and natural form of expression.

La hoja blanca

¡Cuántas veces, la frente en la mano
y en el blanco papel la mirada,
entre el blanco papel y la mente
sorda lucha en secreto se entabla!

Como el mar solicita las velas,
como el aire estimula las olas,
el papel, con su casta blancura,
solicita a la idea y la llama.

Ven—le dice— ; sumido en la mente,
pobre germen, te anulas, te matas;
tenue ser de la nada engendrado
¿no te asusta el volver a la nada?

Ven, amiga; yo soy tu destino,
soy el aire que el aguila aguarda,
soy silencio que aguarda armonías,
soy el mármol que ser quiere estatua.

Soy espera y misterio de cita;
tú la ignota belleza esperada;
soy lo incierto, lo vago, lo amorfo;
tú la línea, el color, la palabra.

Blank Page

How often—when we rest our head
on our hand and scan the blank page—
a soundless combat arises
between the blank page and the mind!

Like the sea inviting sailboats,
like the wind inciting the waves,
the page, pristine and white, chases
after the idea and calls her.

"Come, poor seed," it says, "for buried
in the mind, you'll wither and die;
frail being created from nothing,
don't you fear reverting to it?

"Come, friend, I am your destiny,
I'm the wind the eagle waits for,
I'm silence in wait of music,
I'm marble, in wait of sculpting.

"I'm the mystery of a tryst,
you, the strange beauty I wait for;
I am conjecture, haze, and mist,
you are the line, color, and word.

Yo, mezquino papel, soy el lienzo
donde el Verbo su imagen estampa…
¡Cuántas veces impresa con sangre
en mi nieve su faz deja el alma!

Esperanzas

"I, humble paper, am the cloth
on which the Word stamps its image . . .
How often the soul leaves its face
imprinted in blood on my snow!"

Modern Language Association of America Texts and Translations

Texts

Anna Banti. *"La signorina" e altri racconti*. Ed. and introd. Carol Lazzaro-Weis. 2001.

Adolphe Belot. *Mademoiselle Giraud, ma femme*. Ed and introd. Christopher Rivers. 2002.

Dovid Bergelson. אָפּגאַנג. Ed. and introd. Joseph Sherman. 1999.

Elsa Bernstein. *Dämmerung: Schauspiel in fünf Akten*. Ed. and introd. Susanne Kord. 2003.

Edith Bruck. *Lettera alla madre*. Ed. and introd. Gabriella Romani. 2006.

Isabelle de Charrière. *Lettres de Mistriss Henley publiées par son amie*. Ed. Joan Hinde Stewart and Philip Stewart. 1993.

Isabelle de Charrière. *Trois femmes: Nouvelle de l'Abbé de la Tour*. Ed. and introd. Emma Rooksby. 2007.

François-Timoléon de Choisy, Marie-Jeanne L'Héritier, and Charles Perrault. *Histoire de la Marquise-Marquis de Banneville*. Ed. Joan DeJean. 2004.

Sophie Cottin. *Claire d'Albe*. Ed. and introd. Margaret Cohen. 2002.

Marceline Desbordes-Valmore. *Sarah*. Ed. Deborah Jenson and Doris Y. Kaddish. 2008.

Claire de Duras. *Ourika*. Ed. Joan DeJean. Introd. DeJean and Margaret Waller. 1994.

Şeyh Galip. *Hüsn ü Aşk*. Ed. and introd. Victoria Rowe Holbrook. 2005.

Françoise de Graffigny. *Lettres d'une Péruvienne*. Introd. Joan DeJean and Nancy K. Miller. 1993.

Sofya Kovalevskaya. Нигилистка. Ed. and introd. Natasha Kolchevska. 2001.

Thérèse Kuoh-Moukoury. *Rencontres essentielles*. Introd. Cheryl Toman. 2002.

Juan José Millás. *"Trastornos de carácter" y otros cuentos*. Introd. Pepa Anastasio. 2007.

Emilia Pardo Bazán. *"El encaje roto" y otros cuentos*. Ed. and introd. Joyce Tolliver. 1996.

Rachilde. *Monsieur Vénus: Roman matérialiste*. Ed. and introd. Melanie Hawthorne and Liz Constable. 2004.

Marie Riccoboni. *Histoire d'Ernestine*. Ed. Joan Hinde Stewart and Philip Stewart. 1998.

Eleonore Thon. *Adelheit von Rastenberg*. Ed. and introd. Karin A. Wurst. 1996.

Translations

Anna Banti. *"The Signorina" and Other Stories*. Trans. Martha King and Carol Lazzaro-Weis. 2001.

Adolphe Belot. *Mademoiselle Giraud, My Wife*. Trans. Christopher Rivers. 2002.

Dovid Bergelson. *Descent*. Trans. Joseph Sherman. 1999.

Elsa Bernstein. *Twilight: A Drama in Five Acts*. Trans. Susanne Kord. 2003.

Edith Bruck. *Letter to My Mother*. Trans. Brenda Webster with Gabriella Romani. 2006.

Isabelle de Charrière. *Letters of Mistress Henley Published by Her Friend*. Trans. Philip Stewart and Jean Vaché. 1993.

Isabelle de Charrière. *Three Women: A Novel by the Abbé de la Tour*. Trans. Emma Rooksby. 2007.

François-Timoléon de Choisy, Marie-Jeanne L'Héritier, and Charles Perrault. *The Story of the Marquise-Marquis de Banneville*. Trans. Steven Rendall. 2004.

Sophie Cottin. *Claire d'Albe*. Trans. Margaret Cohen. 2002.

Marceline Desbordes-Valmore. *Sarah*. Trans. Deborah Jenson and Doris Y. Kaddish. 2008.

Claire de Duras. *Ourika*. Trans. John Fowles. 1994.

Şeyh Galip. *Beauty and Love*. Trans. Victoria Rowe Holbrook. 2005.

Françoise de Graffigny. *Letters from a Peruvian Woman*. Trans. David Kornacker. 1993.

Sofya Kovalevskaya. *Nihilist Girl*. Trans. Natasha Kolchevska with Mary Zirin. 2001.

Thérèse Kuoh-Moukoury. *Essential Encounters*. Trans. Cheryl Toman. 2002.

Juan José Millás. *"Personality Disorders" and Other Stories*. Trans. Gregory B. Kaplan. 2007.

Emilia Pardo Bazán. *"Torn Lace" and Other Stories*. Trans. María Cristina Urruela. 1996.

Rachilde. *Monsieur Vénus: A Materialist Novel*. Trans. Melanie Hawthorne. 2004.

Marie Riccoboni. *The Story of Ernestine*. Trans. Joan Hinde Stewart and Philip Stewart. 1998.

Eleonore Thon. *Adelheit von Rastenberg*. Trans. George F. Peters. 1996.

Texts and Translations in One-Volume Anthologies

Modern Italian Poetry. Ed. and trans. Ned Condini. Introd. Dana Renga. 2009.

Modern Urdu Poetry. Ed., introd., and trans. M. A. R. Habib. 2003.

Nineteenth-Century Women's Poetry from France. Ed. Gretchen Schultz. Trans. Anne Atik, Michael Bishop, Mary Ann Caws, Melanie Hawthorne, Rosemary Lloyd, J. S. A. Lowe, Laurence Porter, Christopher Rivers, Schultz, Patricia Terry, and Rosanna Warren. 2008.

Nineteenth-Century Women's Poetry from Spain. Ed. Anna-Marie Aldaz. Introd. Susan Kirkpatrick. Trans. Aldaz and W. Robert Walker. 2009.

Spanish American Modernismo. Ed. Kelly Washbourne. Trans. Washbourne with Sergio Waisman. 2007.